INCANS | AZTECS | MAYANS

A study by
John Holzmann

SONLIGHT

Fifth Edition

Sonlight Curriculum, Ltd.
8042 South Grant Way
Littleton, CO 80122-2705
USA

sonlight.com
main@sonlight.com
(303) 730-6292
Fax: (303) 730-6509

ISBN 978-1-887840-44-6
Printed in the United States of America

Table of Contents

Foreword

You may wonder why I bothered to write my own book about the Incans, Aztecs, and Mayans when there are so many books already available on the market.

That's a fair question.

And the answer, in reverse order of importance, is this:

1) I wanted to save you money. Most books on the Incans, Aztecs, and Mayans are extremely expensive. This book provides far more information at a much lower cost.

2) I wanted to write a book that places the Spanish *conquistadors* in a more accurate light. Most books about the Incan, Aztec, and Mayan cultures seek to glorify them and place them in the best possible light. I am all in favor of such a practice.

However, we should not, at the same time, place the Spanish conquistadors in the worst possible light! Most books on the market teach us that we need to be charitable and "understanding" of the Incans, Aztecs, and Mayans. I agree. It is legitimate for us to seek to understand and be charitable toward those who lack understanding. But were the Incans, Aztecs, and Mayans the only ones who lacked understanding? I believe not. Is it possible that some of the conquistadors lacked understanding as well? Absolutely! Ought we not to be as charitable toward and understanding of these men as we are of and toward the Incans, Aztecs, and Mayans? I am convinced we should be!

3) I wanted to introduce your child(ren) to some basic concepts of anthropology and sociology—all the things that make different cultures unique.

4) I wrote this book with the purpose of providing at least a beginning biblical perspective on the Incan, Aztec, and Mayan cultures as well as of the men who destroyed them.

No book of which I'm aware that deals with the Incans, Aztecs, or Mayans shows even a remote interest in conveying biblical truth. There is a good reason for this. Most modern historians lack a biblical understanding of the world around them. They pretend that all worldviews are equally valid; all worldviews should be looked upon with benign approval. But all worldviews are *not* equally valid, and all worldviews should not be looked upon with benign approval. We must judge all worldviews with a godly (i.e., biblical) judgment. Some beliefs, perspectives, and practices are right and some are wrong. Some are righteous and some unrighteous. We must approve some and condemn the others.

Why Study Other Peoples?

Edwin Abbott, in his classic *Flatland*[1], tries to help us understand what it would be like to live in a very different world: a two-dimensional world in which we are two-dimensional beings in the shape of regular geometric objects. Imagine what a world it would be. "If our friend comes closer to us," says Abbott, "we see his line becomes larger; if he leaves us it becomes smaller: but still he looks like a straight line; be he a Triangle, Square, Pentagon, Hexagon, Circle, what you will—a straight Line he looks and nothing else."

You see things differently in other worlds. What we know as triangles, squares, and so forth in our three-dimensional world, will look like nothing but lines in a two-dimensional world. What we, in our culture, are sure of is that the most normal way of living life on a day-to-day basis may appear as the most foolish behavior in another culture.

Incans, Aztecs & Mayans seeks to introduce readers to three significant cultures that existed on the American continent not so very long ago. Why? Among other reasons: to enable readers to see themselves and their own culture in a new light.

We were brought up in our own culture. We understand our own culture. We believe in our own culture. It is normal for persons born within a culture to view that culture as right, and the way they have been brought up to think and behave as the "normal" way of thinking and behaving.

We see our culture with the eyes of people who are on the inside. There's nothing strange about the way we think or act, is there? The way we think and act is the way everyone thinks and acts, isn't it?

---

[1] New York, NY: Dover Publications, 1952.

By seeing that there are other cultures and other ways of doing things, we can see that our way is not the only way, and maybe—just maybe—our way is not always the best way. Sometimes—perhaps most of the time—we do things better than other people do. But sometimes they may do things better.

By studying other cultures, we open ourselves to the possibility of asking (let alone acquiring accurate answers) about the rightness, wrongness, relative strength or weakness of the way we think and behave in our culture.

*****

There is another good reason for wanting to study other cultures—these three American cultures in particular.

I've discovered, as I prepared this book, that I came to understand Scripture, especially the Old Testament, in a wholly new way. The Incans, Aztecs, and Mayans lived, thought, and acted much more like the ancient Egyptians, Arameans, Moabites, and even Israelites than any modern peoples I know. Their ways of life, their values, their religious systems, their forms of government: I think you'll be amazed at the new insights you gain about the Bible as a result of studying the Incans, Aztecs, and Mayans!

I pray God blesses you and your children as you read this book together.

John Holzmann
May 22, 1996

Incan Territory in South America

Incans

Imagine that you lived way back in the 1400s. Imagine that you lived high up in the Andes Mountains in South America. You would be a citizen of the Incan Empire. You would probably be a farmer. Why? Because that's what the government told you to do.

If you lived in the Incan Empire, the Incan government would tell you what you could do and what you couldn't do.

They would tell you what job you should have and who you could marry. If you wanted to buy some land, build a house, sew clothes, or plant a garden, the government would tell you whether that was all right. They would tell you if you could take a vacation. They would tell you if it was okay to go fishing, hunt a llama, or wear earrings.

The Government: Despotic, Benevolent, and Religious

The Incan government made decisions for the people—big decisions and little decisions. The government controlled every part of the people's lives—even the clothes they could wear and the work they did.

When a government controls people in this way, it is called a *despotic* government. The Incan government was despotic.

But the Incan government did take care of its people. The government wanted to do what was good for its citizens. If you were a citizen of the Incan Empire and were hurt or became sick, the Incan government would make sure you had enough food. They would give you clothes to wear and a good house to live in.

Someone who wants to do good to others is called *benevolent*. The Incan government was benevolent as well as despotic.

There is one more word that describes the Incan government. The Incans and their government were *religious*.[a]

---

[a] When you see a superscript letter, it is meant to refer to a Note For Adults: in the grey boxes throughout the book.

Note For Adults:[a]

To be fully accurate, I should say that the Incan government was *self-consciously* religious. There is no government in the world that is *un*religious. People in modern, Western societies think there is some kind of "separation of religion and state." But, truly, all government—as, indeed, all of life—is religious. It is simply that some governments (and the citizens under the rule of some governments) are more conscious of the religious character of government than are certain other governments and their citizens.

Think about it. Every government in all the history of the world has either thought of itself as being the god and savior of its citizens, or it has acknowledged that there is another god (or there are other gods), and that salvation comes from another source. Every government in all the history of the world has, by its laws and policies, either recognized and promoted worship of the true God, Yahweh, the God of the Bible, or it has promoted worship of some other god. At root, either Yahweh is God, or Mankind is God, or some other god is God. But there can be no neutrality. We must always make a choice.

"If serving [Yahweh] seems undesirable to you," Joshua said to the people of Israel, "then choose for yourselves this day whom you will serve."

It may be the "the gods your forefathers served, . . . or the gods of the Amorites," but you will serve some god(s). So whom will it be? "But as for me and my house," Joshua concluded, "we will serve [Yahweh]" (Joshua 24:15).

Jesus Himself said, "No one can serve two masters. . . . You cannot serve both God and Money" (Matthew 6:24) and, "He who is not with me is against me" (Matthew 12:30).

The Incans thought their king was a god, and that he himself was under the control of a greater god—the Sun.

Because the people believed their king was a god, everything they did was done for the king. So everything they did was important. And everything they did was religious, because it was done for their god, the king. By working for him, they were also serving the Sun.

Colossians 3:23 says, "Whatever you do, work at it with all your heart, as working *for the Lord*, not for men." We Christians are citizens of the kingdom of Yahweh, the God of the Bible. Whatever we do, we are supposed to do it for Yahweh. When we do our work for the Lord Jesus Christ, our God and King, we are serving Yahweh.[b]

Questions
- What does *despotic* mean?
- What does *benevolent* mean?
- How was the Incan government *religious*?

Christians have followed a similar practice. In the case of the New International Version of the Bible, for example, the translators and editors substituted the word "LORD" (all capitals) for the Hebrew word YHWH and "Lord" or "lord" (mixed or lower-case letters) for ADONAI.

To me, this creates major problems. First, the Bible uses both YHWH and ADONAI in its text. If we always use the same word to translate both terms—especially when one of the terms (YHWH) is a proper name and the other (Lord) is not—we either fail to recognize when we are reading the name, or we stop thinking about the meaning of the title ("Lord" means "master," one who has authority and must be obeyed). This leads to further problems when, for instance, Yahweh commands us to "make [His] name known." How do we make His name known if we never use His name? And what do we do with such statements as David's, when he approached Goliath: "You come against me with sword and spear and javelin, but I come against you in the name of [—look it up!] Almighty, the God of the armies of Israel..."

Though Yahweh is lord, His name is not "LORD" (however you wish to capitalize it). Nor is His name "God" (either capitalized or uncapitalized). Yahweh is Yahweh and He is the Lord and He is the only true God!

There are false gods who make various claims to sovereignty and power. They have names. But we worship the true God, Yahweh. Let us name His Name!

Learning from History

Around the world today, only a few people groups live the way the Incans did. The way a people group lives is called their *culture*. The culture of the Incans was very different from the culture of most people groups today.

But if we look carefully at the Incan culture, I believe we can learn from their way of life. We can learn some things we *should* do, and many things we should *not* do.^c

First, let us think about something the Incans did that we, also, should do.

The Incans obeyed their god.

The Incans' god was a false god. The Incan king was not Yahweh! But we can still learn something from the Incans. They obeyed their king in everything he told them to do. Yahweh tells us to obey *Him* in everything He tells us to do.

Most people today do not obey Yahweh. But we need to read His Word, listen to Him, and obey Him in every area of our lives—just like the Incans obeyed their god.

Here is something else we can learn from the Incans.

The Incans served a despotic government—a government that controlled everything they did. But it was a *human* government. The Incans thought their king was a god, but he was really a human

Note For Adults:[c]

Did you ever stop to think: We can learn good things from good examples *and* we can learn good things from bad examples!

Sometimes we can learn best by looking at the wise and good things other people do. Sometimes we can learn from the foolish and evil things they do. We see wise and good behavior and we say, "That is really smart!" —Look at how Solomon argues in Proverbs 6:6, for example. "Go to the ant, you sluggard; consider its ways and be wise!"

Then there are those times we see people doing evil and foolish things and we realize, "That's not what I want to do!" Consider, for example, how Solomon argues in Proverbs 1:10-17. There he tells his son to stay away from certain kinds of people because "their feet rush into sin, they are swift to shed innocent blood. . . ." "*See* what kinds of things these people do? *See* how they end up? *You* don't want to end up like them, do you?" he asks.

We can learn in both these ways from other peoples and other cultures. We can see what they did right, and we can see what they did wrong. And we can decide that the right way is better.

being. Yahweh is despotic, too. He tells us how we should live our lives. But Yahweh is the true God. That makes all the difference in the world!

Yahweh knows everything. He knows what is good and what is bad. He knows what is helpful and what is not helpful. He knows what will give us life, joy, and peace, and He knows what will bring death, unhappiness, bitterness, and battles. But leaders who are human may know many things, but they don't know everything.

Yahweh is perfect. He is holy and righteous. There is no sin in Him. But human leaders are not perfect. Even if they are benevolent, they are not perfectly righteous like Yahweh is.

Living under the control of a despotic human government is very difficult. But living under the control of Yahweh is easy. Jesus said, "[His] yoke is easy and [His] burden is light" (Matthew 11:30). When we live our lives for Yahweh and obey Him, we have the life, joy, and peace that only He can give.

Just as individual people need to obey Yahweh, governments need to obey Yahweh, too. But oftentimes governments have disobeyed Yahweh. They have tried to do more and more things—things that Yahweh never gave them permission to do. Because of this, in the last hundred years, governments have caused more death and sadness than ever before in history.

Questions
• Why is it useful to study other cultures?
• How can it be good to study another culture *even if the people do evil*?
• Is it *ever* possible to have a truly *good* despotic government? Why or why not?

Tavantinsuyu

The Incans called their country Tavantinsuyu (TAH-vahn-tin-SOO-yoo), which means "the Four Quarters of the World."

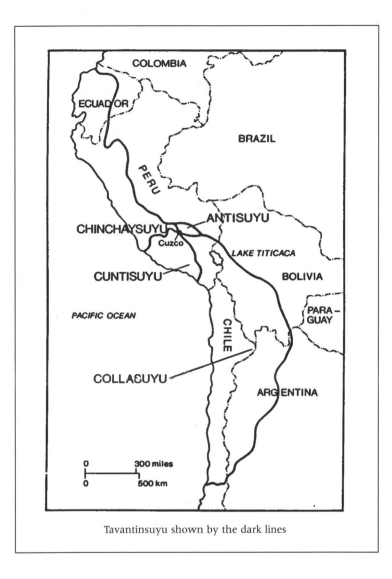

Tavantinsuyu shown by the dark lines

Part of it was located where Peru is today. It was a long, narrow country, stretching almost 3,000 miles. That's farther than the distance between New York City, NY and Los Angeles, CA or between Vancouver, BC and Halifax, NS. The Incan Empire covered almost the entire western edge of South America.

The Incan Empire, Tavantinsuyu, was divided into four parts. (See the map on this page.) The capital city, *Cuzco* (COOS-coh), was connected by roadways to each of the four parts of the empire.

Tavantinsuyu began sometime in the early 1100s. In about A.D. 1450[d] it was the greatest it had ever been. Yet, barely 100 years later, the country fell apart. By A.D. 1550 the Incan Empire had disappeared.

Note For Adults:[d]

A.D. stands for *Anno Domini*, "the year of our Lord." A.D. is meant to contrast with B.C., "before Christ." But it contrasts with something else, too. It contrasts with "any god but Christ, any god but Yahweh." And so, secular-minded historians now either leave off any mention of A.D., or they speak of C.E. and B.C.E.—the "common era" and "before [the] common era." As I believe in Jesus Christ, wish to assert His crown rights over all creation, and look forward to the day when, in the fullest sense of the term, "the kingdom of this world [will] become the kingdom of our Lord and of His Christ" (Revelation 11:15): I unabashedly and deliberately join other Christian historians down through the centuries who have used the term A.D. when dating events after the birth of Christ.

Legend of Beginnings

There is a story that tells how the Incan Empire began. The Incans believed that this legend was true.

According to the legend, the Sun sent two of his children, a son and a daughter, to live on the earth. These two children were gods, like the Sun. They were sent to earth to teach human beings how to live.

The two young gods settled in the place that would later become the city of Cuzco, and people from all around came to learn from the gods. The male god taught the men how to plant crops. The female god taught the women how to weave cloth and spin yarn.

The people were very thankful for the help they received from the gods. To show their thankfulness, they built the city of Cuzco.

According to the legend, the gods supposedly came to earth in the 1100s. According to history, the Spaniards arrived almost 400 years later, and destroyed the Incan Empire.

Question
• What did the Incans believe about where they came from?

☀☺☀☺☀☺☀☺☀☺☀☺☀☺☀☺☀

Cuzco

The city of Cuzco was the capital of the Incan Empire. It was divided into four parts—just like the whole country was divided into four parts. People from the four areas of the country lived in the parts of Cuzco that were closest to their home provinces. So, if you came from the southeast province, you would live in the southeast part of Cuzco.

People from the four parts of the country could easily get to Cuzco, because Cuzco was in the middle of the country. In fact, that's how Cuzco got its name. Cuzco means "navel" or "belly-button." It was the "navel" of the Incan Empire because it was in the middle of the empire.

Question
• Describe the city of Cuzco.

☀☺☀☺☀☺☀☺☀☺☀☺☀☺☀☺☀

A Centralized Civilization

The king of the Incan Empire was the *High Inca*. The High Inca lived in Cuzco. But he knew what was going on in the whole country. Whenever something important happened, somebody would tell him about it. And whenever the High Inca made a decision, his decision was communicated to everyone in the empire.

How was this communication possible? The Incans didn't have telephones or cars. But they did have roads. And people could travel the roads by foot.

Travel and Communication

Tavantinsuyu had two major roads that went from north to south. One of these roads was on the eastern side of the country, and the other was on the western side.

The eastern road went through the mountains. This was the high road.

It took a lot of work to build the high road. Long portions of the road were cut out of the sides of the mountains. When the road builders came to a cliff, they cut stairs into it, and the stairs became part of the road. In some places, the road was so high up in the mountains that it was covered by snow all year round.

The western road was near the ocean. It was the low road.

There weren't any mountains right by the ocean, but there was a lot of sand. The road builders piled dirt on top of the sand so it would stay above any water that came up on the beach.

The Incans built clay walls on both sides of the low road. They also planted trees and shrubs along the

Incan Trail, part of the old high road

sides. People could smell the fragrant shrubs and enjoy the beauty as they traveled along the road.

Both the high and low roads had rest stations built every ten to twelve miles.

With such fine roads, you'd think the Incans would have traveled quite a bit. But very few Incans ever left their hometowns. In fact, though the Incan Empire was right next to the Pacific Ocean, the Incans didn't ship anything across the ocean. They didn't do any trading with other countries.

So who used the roads in Tavantinsuyu? Mostly the government. The roads made it possible for the High Inca to find out what was going on in the empire. The roads also made it possible for messages from the High Inca to be communicated to other parts of the empire.

Question
• What was so amazing about the Incan roads?

🌟 ☺ 🌟 ☺ 🌟 ☺ 🌟 ☺ 🌟 ☺ 🌟 ☺ 🌟 ☺ 🌟 ☺ 🌟

Chasquis

Besides the rest stations, the Incans built small buildings every five miles along the major roads. These buildings were for the *chasquis* (CHASS keec).

Chasquis were men who could run fast for long distances. In fact, running was their job! The chasquis carried small packages for the government and passed along important messages.

The chasquis delivered their messages and packages by running in relays. One chasqui would run five miles from his little building to the next little building. He would pass on the message or the package to the next chasqui, who would then run the next five miles to another chasqui. Together, the chasquis could carry a message as far as 150 miles in one day!

Sometimes government messages were sent by word of mouth. Each chasqui would have to memorize the message, and then pass the message on to the next chasqui.

Other times, messages were sent by *quipus* (KEE-poos), a special type of writing that used ropes instead of paper and ink.

Sometimes the High Inca would give a chasqui a thread from the crimson fringe he wore around his head. When the High Inca sent this thread along with a message, it meant that the message was very important. The person who received the message would know that it came directly from the High Inca himself.[1]

People in Incan society had to wear the kind of clothing that the government told them to wear. It was as if everyone had his or her own uniform. This helped the Incans to know who every person was and what that person's job was. If they knew what job a person had, they then would know how to act around that person.

The chasquis wore clothing that was very different from everyone else so regular citizens of the empire treated the chasquis very differently than they treated other people. The chasquis were important!

Besides messages, chasquis sometimes carried fish, fruit, small animals, and other foods to be served fresh to the king. The chasquis were truly a "Federal Express" system for the Incan government!

Because of the roads and the chasquis, the High Inca knew almost immediately whenever anything happened in his empire. And because he knew what was happening, he could respond in the right way. If any enemies tried to attack Tavantinsuyu, the High Inca would hear about it quickly and be able to decide what to do to defend the country.

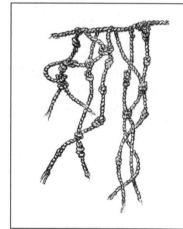

The Incans had no system of writing. But for counting, and to help them remember things, they used the *quipu*—a number of different colored, knotted cords tied to a main cord. The position and color of each knot determined the meaning.

---

[1] The thread acted among the Incans much as a king's seal used to act in Europe or the way our signatures act on contracts and bills written today. The signature says, "This document is authentic. I wrote it. You can trust that it says what I said."

Questions

• Who were the *chasquis*?
• What was a *quipu*?
• What two things helped make Cuzco the center of Incan civilization?

☼☺☼☺☼☺☼☺☼☺☼☺☼☺☼☺☼

Barter Society

One of the main reasons the Incans didn't travel very much was because they had no money. Why didn't they have any money? Because no one had ever thought of it!

Instead of working, being paid for their work with money, and then paying money for the items they wanted to buy, the Incans traded things with each other. This kind of trading is called *bartering*.

Do people in our society ever barter? If one person trades what he has for something someone else has, they are bartering. If you trade a stamp collection for a bicycle, you are bartering. If you trade three used books for one new book, you are bartering. If you trade your work in the yard for a trip to the zoo, you are bartering.

But even though you may barter like this once in a while, America is not a *barter society*. Someone still has to buy the stamps or the bicycle or the books in the first place, and someone still has to pay money to get into the zoo.

In Incan society, nobody paid money for anything. Incan society was a barter society.

The problem with a barter society is that it is difficult to trade. You might want to trade your twenty bushels of apples for my cow. But how would you haul your twenty bushels of apples over to my house? And what happens if I don't want your apples? Maybe I like apples well enough, but I just can't imagine eating twenty bushels of them before they go rotten. Or maybe I don't even like apples. Then what?

What if apples are the only thing you have to trade? Will we make a trade? And even if we do make the trade, it may take me several hours to get my cow to you.

In a barter society, if we live far apart from one another, we probably won't trade with each other. Even if there is a nice road between us, it would be too hard to carry our goods or herd our animals a long distance. If people in my town produce most of the same goods that people in your town produce, it will almost always be easier for me to trade with people in my own town.

So, as nice as the roads might be, we would not use them very much.

Question
• What is a *barter* society?

☀☺☀☺☀☺☀☺☀☺☀☺☀☺☀☺☀

Social Structure

Roads connected Cuzco with the different parts of the empire. The chasquis made communication possible between Cuzco and the different parts of the empire. But something else was actually much more important to Incan civilization than either the roads or the chasquis.

That more important thing was a person—the High Inca.

The High Inca was the head of the Incan government. He was the most important person in the Incan religion. In fact, for the Incan people, their whole lives centered around the High Inca. They believed that without him, the world would come to an end.

The High Inca

In Western countries, many people think that religion should not be a part of government. They think that teachers should not teach what God teaches. They don't want students to pray in school. And they don't think Christianity has anything to do with business.

According to many Western leaders today, religion isn't important. If you want to be religious, that's your business, as long as you don't let it affect anyone else. You can talk to God in private if you want, but don't talk about God in public.

That's *not* the way it used to be in Western Europe or in the United States. That's *not* the way it is in Muslim countries. That's *not* the way it was in Tavantinsuyu. And that's *certainly not* the way God says it should be!

For the Incans, everything was religious. Everything they did, they did for the High Inca. All their wealth, all their skills—everything—was given to him.

The Incans believed that the High Inca was sent by the Sun to tell them how they should live. They also believed that the High Inca was a god himself.

Every few years, the High Inca would travel around the empire. When he traveled, he didn't walk. Instead, his servants would carry him on a special chair that was set on poles. The servants would carry

On certain festivals, the priests would remove the bodies of the High Incas from the temple and bring them out to the Cuzco public square so they could be paraded around. From the *Codex Florentino*

the poles, so the High Inca could have a comfortable ride in his chair. This type of chair on poles is called a litter.[2]

The Incan people watched carefully when they saw the High Inca's litter coming. They usually didn't see the High Inca himself, because his chair was covered by a curtain. If the High Inca happened

---

[2] Many cultures' princes and priests have used litters in the past.

to lift the curtain on his litter so that the people could see him, they would quickly bow down and bless him.

If he happened to actually walk somewhere or stand on the ground, the people considered the place where he walked or stood to be holy ground. They would build shrines to help them remember the days when their god, the king, appeared before them.

The High Inca was also the chief priest and worship leader. The Incans believed that he was the only one who could make all their sacrifices and prayers worth anything.[e]

Note For Adults:[e]

The High Inca was the Incans' *Prophet*. According to the Incan religion, it was the High Inca who told the people what the Sun wanted them to do.

The High Inca was also the Incans' High *Priest*. He led them in their sacrifices and their worship of the Sun.

Finally, the High Inca was the Incans' *King*. He ruled the Incans. And he made sure they did what the Sun wanted them to do.

The Incans were sure that they could not do what the Sun wanted them to do if they didn't have a High Inca. And what would happen if they didn't do what the Sun wanted them to do? The Sun might stop shining! Then all life on earth would stop! The earth would become cold, the plants would stop growing, and no one would live.

So everything depended on the High Inca. If the High Inca didn't do his job, then the Sun wouldn't do his job either. And if the Sun didn't do his job, the world would end.

Jesus is our Prophet, Priest, and King. We are supposed to listen to Jesus to learn what Yahweh wants. We are supposed to turn to Jesus as our great High Priest. And we are supposed to obey Jesus, because He is our true King.

The High Inca tried to be a Prophet, Priest, and King. But the Bible tells us that Jesus is the *true* Prophet, Priest, and King. May we serve Jesus better than the Incans served their High Inca!

The High Inca served his people in other ways. He was the commander of the army. As commander, he did not stay back in a safe place during battles. He went with his troops and actually led them into battle.

The High Inca also made laws, decided who the judges would be, and told the people what taxes to pay.

The Coya

The High Inca's wife was called a *Coya* (COY-uh). The Incans believed that the High Inca came from the Sun, and the Coya represented the Moon. They believed that the High Inca was a god, and the Coya was a goddess. Sometimes when the High Inca was away on a journey, the Coya ruled Tavantinsuyu.

Besides the Coya, a High Inca had many slave-wives. These slave-wives were called *concubines*. But only the Coya was considered to be a goddess.

When a High Inca died, one of his sons would become the High Inca in his place. A High Inca could have many, many sons (because of his many concubines). But the sons of the concubines did not become High Incas. It was only the eldest son of the Coya who would become the next High Inca.

Question
• Who was the *Coya*? What did she do?

The High Inca's Wealth

The High Inca had lots of magnificent palaces. These palaces were built all over the country.

On the outside, they didn't look very fancy. They were low buildings, with just one story, and they were built of large stones. But on the inside, they were beautiful! The walls were covered with gold and silver ornaments. The Incans cut niches in the walls to hold even more gold and silver—gold and silver figures of animals and plants.

Everything the High Inca used was made from gold or silver: even his chairs, tables, and eating utensils.

Along with all the gold and silver, the High Inca also used richly colored fabrics. They were special fabrics and special colors. The common people were never allowed to wear those same fabrics or colors.

The High Inca was always rich, but he never got any of that wealth from his father. There's a reason for that. It had to do with what happened when a High Inca died.

The Incans believed their High Incas would one day return to life and, when they did, they would want to use all their belongings again. So when a High Inca died, the Incan people and the new High Inca abandoned all the palaces, except one. They wanted to make sure the High Inca could use his palaces when he came back to life.

Not only did the Incans abandon the palaces; they abandoned all the belongings in the palaces as well—the furniture, the sculptures, and all the High Inca's treasures.

The one palace the Incans still used after a High Inca died was in Yucay, a valley about 12 miles from Cuzco.

What Happened When the High Inca Died

When a High Inca died, the Incans would remove his intestines from his body. They buried the intestines in a special tomb in the temple of Tampu, about 15 miles from Cuzco. The Incans also buried lots of gold, silver, and jewelry along with the High Inca's intestines.

Next they would sacrifice all his servants and concubines on top of the tomb. Sometimes they would kill as many as a thousand servants and concubines.

The Incans would embalm the High Inca's body to keep it from decaying. Then they would place it in the Temple of the Sun at Cuzco.

They placed all the bodies of the dead High Incas and Coyas in this temple. The bodies were seated on golden chairs, with their hands crossed over their chests and their heads facing downward. The High Incas' bodies were seated on the right side of the temple;

the Coyas' bodies were on the left side, facing the bodies of the High Incas.

When a High Inca died, the Incans would mourn for him for a whole year.

Questions

- What did the Incans believe about life after death?
- After a High Inca died, what did they do with his palaces? What did they do with his belongings? What did they do with his body?
- Why do you think the Incans did the things they did after the High Inca died?

🌟 ☺ 🌟 ☺ 🌟 ☺ 🌟 ☺ 🌟 ☺ 🌟 ☺ 🌟 ☺ 🌟 ☺ 🌟

The High Inca's Education

Men called *amautas* (ah-MOW-tahs) were the Incans' wise men. They taught the sons of the High Inca how to do all the religious ceremonies and how to fight in wars.

When a son of the High Inca turned 16, he underwent tests to see how strong he was. He had to show his strength by wrestling, boxing, running, and even going without food for a while. The young men were also tested on how well they could fight. For the purposes of the test, they used weapons that would not cause too much pain. The tests lasted for 30 days.

When a son of the High Inca passed his tests, he was allowed to become a *huaracu* (wah-RAH-coo). His ears were pierced, and then the hole was slowly stretched. Larger and larger things would be placed in the hole, until finally it was stretched so much that a large pendant could be put through. By the time the stretching was finished, the High Inca's earlobes almost touched his shoulders.

Besides having their ears pierced, the new huaracus also received sandals for their feet and a special girdle for their loins. Their elders also placed colorful flowers and evergreen leaves on their heads.

The eldest son of the Coya was treated specially, because he would someday become the next High Inca. Once he became a huaracu, he was allowed to join the group of men who helped his father rule the country. He was also given a special headdress made of yellow wool, with tassels on it. The very soft yellow wool came from a vicuna, an animal similar to a llama.

Questions
• What was an *amauta*?
• What was a *huaracu*?

🌞☺🌞☺🌞☺🌞☺🌞☺🌞☺🌞☺🌞☺🌞

Other Nobles

I am using the name *Incans*ᶜ to refer to all the people of the Incan Empire. Actually, they didn't call themselves Incans. They were just the people of Tavantinsuyu. But it is easier to say *Incans* than *Tavantinsuyuans*.

The name *Inca* was a special title given to only a few of the Incan people. The *Incas* were the noblemen. They became noblemen because they descended from the very first High Inca. So they were cousins or distant cousins of the later High Incas.

All the Incas wore special clothes, different from the clothes of anyone else in the empire. They spoke a special language, too, and lived apart from the common people. Most of them lived at the prince's court. They ate with him and spent their time with him.

These noblemen were the only ones who could serve as priests. If they did not serve as priests, they served as commanders in the army.

Besides the Incas, there was another class of noblemen. The leaders of nations that the Incans had conquered became noblemen in the Incan Empire. So did all of their descendants. These leaders and their descendants were called *Curacas* (coo-RAW-cahs).

Every once in a while the High Inca would invite the Curacas to visit Cuzco so they could tell him what they had been doing. Otherwise they lived in their hometowns.

If Curaca boys wanted to be educated, they had to go to Cuzco. Most Curaca boys did want an education. The High Inca required them to come to Cuzco for their education so that they would learn to respect the Incan way of life. He wanted the Curacas to always be faithful to serve their High Inca.

Question
• Who were the *Curacas*?

☀☺☀☺☀☺☀☺☀☺☀☺☀☺☀☺☀☺☀

Note For Adults:[f]

Today when most people talk about the *Incans,* they think they are talking about the people who lived in Tavantinsuyu. But the common people who lived in Tavantinsuyu never referred to themselves as Incas. Only *Tavantinsuyuan* (TAH-vahn-tin-soo-YOO-ahn) nobles were ever called Incas. In other words, the king, his sons, and grandsons were called Incas. Everyone else was . . . just someone who lived in Tavantinsuyu!

But since the word *Tavantinsuyu* is so difficult to pronounce, I'm going to follow the example of others and use the title of their king to refer to all of the Tavantinsuyuans together. When speaking of the Tavantinsuyuan nobles, I will speak of the *High Inca* and the *Incas* (the *High Inca* is the high king; the *Incas* are the descendants of the king). When speaking of the common people or the Tavantinsuyuans in general, I will speak of the *Incan people*, or the *Incans*.

The Incan Government

The Incans had one of the most highly developed governments of all time.

At the top was the High Inca. Under him were four noblemen who ruled the four provinces of the empire.

Under these four noblemen there were governors. Each of these governors ruled many thousands of people.

Under the governors were officials who ruled thousands, and under them were officials who ruled hundreds. Finally there were overseers who supervised ten foremen apiece. And each of the foremen supervised ten peasants.

When you counted everyone—men, women, and children—one out of every ten Incans was a government official! There were about nine million people in the Incan Empire by the early 1500s. That's a lot of people and a lot of officials!

The Incans had very few laws, but those few laws were strict. In most cases, the penalty for breaking a law was death. For instance, if you stole something, the penalty was death. If you spoke against the Sun or the High Inca, the penalty was death.

In some cases, the law was not so harsh. If you removed landmarks, or turned water away from your neighbor's garden into your own, or burned someone's house, you would be beaten severely but probably not killed.

Each community had its own judge. The judge could handle easy cases. But if a case was too difficult for the local judge to deal with, he could pass it on to a higher judge. Usually the higher judge was a governor.

The Economy

With so many government officials, the Incans' lives were very carefully controlled. The government controlled the Incans' work and land and what they produced on the land. This was all part of their *economy*. The government controlled the economy.

Government-Controlled

In the Incan Empire, whenever someone was born or someone died, a government official recorded that information. Once a year, the local recorders gave this information to the top government officials in Cuzco. The Incan officials then used the information to decide what work each person should do. They also used it to divide the farmland evenly.

The Incan government divided the farmland into three parts. Remember that the country was already divided into four quarters.

(See the map on page 15.) The three parts of the farmland were not like the four quarters of the empire. The farmland was not divided into three huge pieces of land. Rather, within each of the four quarters of the empire there were lots of little bits of farmland. Some of the pieces of land were set aside for the Sun, some for the High Inca, and some for the common people.

Now, of course, the Sun didn't shine on just the land set apart for it. And the High Inca didn't go around and cultivate the land set apart for him. No, it was the common people who farmed *all* of the land. But the crops grown on one part were for the Sun, crops on the second section were for the High Inca, and crops on the third were for the rest of the people.

The crops grown on the Sun's land supported the work of the temple, the priests, and the worship.

The crops grown on the High Inca's property supported the government. The government made sure that widows, orphans, old people, and sick people had food to eat.

And the crops grown on the people's portion supported everyone else.

The common people lived near their relatives—the people of their own clan. Their land was divided by clan. The amount of land that one clan had depended on how many people were in the clan. Bigger clans were given more land. A married couple received a certain portion. Children received smaller amounts. Daughters received a single portion. Sons enjoyed double portions.

Because babies were always being born and older children and adults were dying, the government divided the land again at the end of each year so every clan would always have a fair share.

The government officials kept track of many things. They counted the people and they also kept track of the quality of the soil. They wanted to know if the soil was still good for producing crops.

Questions
• What is a *clan*?
• What kinds of information did the government officials collect each year? Why did they want this information?

- Who received the crops grown on the three different parts of the farmland?

☀☺☀☺☀☺☀☺☀☺☀☺☀☺☀☺☀

Occupations

Most Incan men served as farmers. A few learned how to do metal work, mining, construction, and other things. There were not many builders or metal workers, but those who had these skills were very good at what they did.

The Incans' buildings were amazing. They were usually made of large, heavy stones, so they would last a long time. The stones were cut just right, so they would fit together very closely. In fact, the stones fit together so closely that you could not slip a knife blade between them!

Because Incan buildings were built so well, many of them

Incan hut

are still standing today. It has been hundreds of years since they were built, and earthquakes have destroyed other types of buildings near them. Even buildings that were built centuries later have fallen down. But the work of skillful Incan builders is still visible today.

The rooms in Incan buildings were not connected to each other. Instead, they opened into courtyards. To get from one room to another, you had to go out into the courtyard first, then into another room. The Incans had no windows. Light had to come through the doorway!

The buildings never had any decorations on the outside. But sometimes the builders would make the edges of the stones very

Incan wall: see how carefully the stones were cut?

smooth, or even polish them. Then the stones could catch the sunlight, and the light would make patterns as it reflected off the stones.

The Incans made most of their tools from stone or copper. Eventually they learned how to mix copper with tin to make bronze. The bronze was very hard. But it seems the Incans did not use bronze to make weapons.

Question

• What are some of the most interesting things you have learned about the Incans' buildings?

Agriculture

Only common people worked as farmers. The noblemen never farmed.

Every year, the peasant men first had to farm the lands that belonged to the Sun. They had to do this so that the priests would have food to eat. Then they had to work the plots that provided food for old and sick people, widows, and orphans. Finally, they could work their own lands.

If they had any extra time left over, they couldn't just do what they wanted. They had to spend their extra time doing whatever else the High Inca wanted them to do.

Farming Techniques

The Incans were surprisingly good farmers.

Near the ocean, in the lowlands, the Incans used canals and underground water pipes to water their fields. Long water pipes like this are called *aqueducts*. One aqueduct was over 400 miles long!

In places that were higher than the water level, it was impossible to pipe water to the fields. But the Incans found a solution to this problem. In these areas, they sometimes dug out a huge area of land so that the ground would be as low as the water level. Then they planted seed in the dug out area and were able to water their crops. Some of these lots were fifteen to twenty feet deep and as big as a football field!

In most places around the world, if you dig down a few inches, the soil is very poor. It will hardly grow a thing. But the Incans found a solution to this problem, too. They improved the soil with fertilizers. Their two favorite fertilizers were sardine heads and bird droppings.

One man who saw what they did said that "along the entire coast from Arequipa to Taracapa the only fertiliser used was that of the seagulls, unbelievably large flocks of which were to be found there. These birds, both large and small, live on islands not far from the shore, which are covered with such quantities of their droppings that they look like mountains of snow."

In the highlands, further away from the coast, the farmers had different problems. How do you plant a crop on the side of a mountain? Again, the Incans found a solution to their problem. They cut giant steps, called *terraces*, into the sides of the mountains. By making terraces like this, the Incans could have little bits of flat farmland all up and down the side of a steep mountain.

One thing the Incans did *not* know about was the plow. Modern farmers use plows to loosen the soil and make it ready for planting. The Incans made a long hole called a *furrow*. Six or eight strong men would drag a sharply pointed stake across the ground to make the furrow. Then they could plant seeds in this long hole.

Terraces up the side of the mountain

Questions
• What did Incan farmers do to make their crops grow?
• What is a *terrace*?
• What is a *furrow*?
• What is a *plow*?

☀☺☀☺☀☺☀☺☀☺☀☺☀☺☀☺☀

Products
Crops

Because Tavantinsuyu stretched from the ocean to the mountains, it had both lowlands and highlands. These different areas had totally different climates. One crop might grow well in one climate, but not very well in another climate. So the Incans grew different crops in different parts of the country.

People in the lowlands grew *cassava*. The root of the cassava plant is what we use nowadays to make tapioca. Early in their history the

Incans also grew bananas. Later, they stopped growing bananas and grew *maize* instead. Maize is another word for corn.

Most people today use maize to make bread but the Incans made cornbread only for festivals. Most of the time they used the cornstalks to make a sweet syrup, and they used the corn itself to make beer.

People in the highlands grew potatoes.

In the middle areas, between the lowlands and highlands, the Incans grew a desert plant called *maguey* (MAG-way), which has thick leaves and is a good source of fiber. They grew tobacco to use as a medicine, and they grew a grain called *quinoa* (KEEN-wah). Quinoa is like rice. They also grew *coca*. The Incans used coca leaves like Westerners use coffee today. It helped them to stay awake and to work longer. It made them feel good and made them less hungry. But the Incans didn't *drink* coca like Westerners drink coffee. They *chewed* it. Today many of the Incans' descendants still chew dried coca leaves mixed with lime, just like their ancestors did.

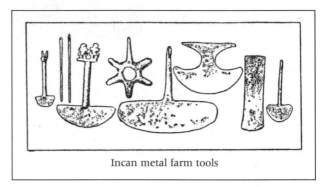

Incan metal farm tools

Coca is the stuff from which cocaine is made. In 1858 a scientist named Albert Niemann figured out how to get the cocaine out of coca leaves. After that, people in other parts of the world started using pure cocaine instead of chewing the leaves.

Meat

The Incans ate very little meat. The main reason was because they were only allowed to hunt once each year. And the one time they did hunt was planned by the government. Every year the hunt was held in a different province.

Hunting party

During the hunt, a man was allowed to catch as much as he could. Then he had to bring whatever he caught to a certain place and turn it over to the government. Everything that everyone caught was divided up and shared with people throughout the empire.

The men hunted animals like deer, *llamas* (LAW-muhs), and a certain kind of sheep that had coarse wool. They could catch as many of these animals as they could, but they could only kill the deer and the sheep. They couldn't kill the llamas.

After the hunt, they turned the animal skins into leather. The meat they cut into thin slices and made into *charqui* (CHAR-kee). This is the same as jerky—meat that is preserved by drying.[3]

Textiles

The Incans would capture between 30,000 and 40,000 llamas during the annual hunt. But the High Inca owned all the llamas in Tavantinsuyu. It was against the law to hunt llamas for meat. And the penalty for breaking this law was death.

So what did they do with the thousands of llamas that they caught?

Llama

Llamas are similar to camels but are small and woolly. The Incans

---

[3] The word *charqui* is very similar to our modern English word *jerky* (as in beef jerky). That is because jerky is what used to be called charqui!

sheared the llamas to get their wool. Then they released the animals. The government stored the wool and later distributed it to the people.

Each year, certain government officials traveled throughout the empire to make sure every family had enough wool for their clothing. The women made fabric from the wool of the llamas. Every Incan woman who was healthy enough to work had to make fabric for her family.

The officials gave the llama wool to the women. Then they came back later to make sure the women were producing as much cloth as they were supposed to . . . and that the cloth was as good as the government demanded.

Besides llama wool, Incan women used the maguey plant to make a different type of fabric. In the lowlands, they also used cotton to make fabric.

Other Parts of the Economy

The Incans dug mines in the ground to find metal. All these mines and all the metal found in them belonged to the High Inca.

The Incans sent some of the metal to Cuzco. They sent some of the crops they grew on the High Inca's lands and they sent some of the weapons and other goods they produced as well. They sent all of these things to Cuzco so the priests and Incas could use them.

However, of all the food, metal, weapons, and other goods that the people made for the Inca, most were stored in large stone buildings. They were kept in case of an emergency.

Thus, for example, if there was a famine in the land, the people wouldn't starve. They could eat the food that was stored in the storehouses. If the Incan army suddenly needed more

Incan pottery: Compare their pottery to the Aztecs' and Mayans'

supplies, they could get them from the storehouses. You could find many of these large buildings throughout the countryside.

The common people paid all the taxes. The nobles, priests, and public employees did not pay any taxes.

Questions
- What main crops did the Incans grow?
- In the United States and most other Western countries today, it is against the law to own or use drugs that are made from coca leaves. But coca wasn't always against the law. When Coca Cola™ was first produced, it had coca in it. That's where it got its name. Think about this, and think about any passages in the Bible that might tell us what to do about this.

  Do you think it should be against the law to own coca leaves or to chew coca leaves? Why or why not?

  If you think it should be against the law, should there also be laws against drinking coffee or other drinks that have caffeine in them? Why or why not?
- What is *charqui*?
- What three types of fabric did Incan women make?

☀☺☀☺☀☺☀☺☀☺☀☺☀☺☀☺☀

Social Security, But No Opportunities

The Incan people could not do whatever they wanted to do or be whatever they wanted to be. They had to be whatever their parents had been, and do what their parents had done. Most men were farmers, and their sons would be farmers, too. Girls would grow up to be mothers and cloth-makers.

Nobody even thought of being anything else. They knew they would do the same kind of work that their parents did. This is what the government told people to do. And this is what seemed normal to everyone. It was "the way things are and ought to be."

The Incans did not try to change the way things were. They did not care about progress, or making things better. They just cared about staying alive . . . and serving the Sun and the High Inca.

In our society we are happy that we can choose what we want to do. As Christians, we believe that God has given each one of us special gifts to do special jobs for His glory. If we use the gifts and skills God has given us, we will help others to have a better life. And we will see progress in our own lives, too.

If you asked an Incan what he thought about his work, he would happily tell you: "Because we all work together, no one ever goes hungry. Even if there is a famine, our High Inca has stored enough food so that none of us ever goes hungry."

The Incans were born, and they died. While they were alive, they did not get richer or poorer. They stayed the same. They didn't even think of the possibility of things being different. They believed that the way they lived was the way life was supposed to be. They knew that if they did their work, they would have enough food to eat, even if there was a famine.

What more could they want?

Question

- This section of the book closes with the question: "What more could they want?" Talk about it. Do you think you might have been happy as an Incan? Why or why not?

🌞☺🌞☺ 🌞☺🌞☺🌞☺🌞☺ 🌞☺🌞☺🌞

Cultural Goal: Changing Other Nations

The Incan people didn't expect their personal lives to change. They expected everything to stay the same. But as a nation, the Incans wanted to change the nations around them. They wanted the people in other nations to live just like they did—to worship the Sun and to serve the High Inca.

This is how they would try to change another nation.

First, the High Inca would talk to the leaders of the other nation. He would try to convince the leaders that the Incan way of life was best. And the Incan people themselves tried to show the other nation what a great life they had as Incans.

If the people of the other nation did not want to live like Incans, the High Inca and other government officials would give gifts to the other nation's leaders. They would give the gifts, and ask, "Don't you want to become Incans?"[g]

Note For Adults:[g]

The Incans' goal was very similar to the one our God, Yahweh, has given us. Jesus has told us to "make disciples of all nations, baptizing them in the name of the Father [Yahweh] and of the Son [Jesus] and of the Holy Spirit, and teaching them to obey everything" (Matthew 28:19-20). Our entire lives are to be directed toward Yahweh's glory. We are to extend the borders of *His* Kingdom among all nations and to encourage all the peoples of the world to obey *His* ways.

In spite of the Incans' sweet talk and gifts, the other nations' leaders knew that the next step would be war. They knew that if they did not do what the Incans wanted, the Incans would attack them.

The leaders of the other nation also knew that the Incans were the most powerful empire in the region. If the Incans went to war against them, it would be a terrible battle. And the Incans were almost sure to win.

Rahab told the Israelite spies when they stayed at her house in Jericho, "A great fear of you has fallen on us, so that all who live in this country are melting in fear because of you. We have heard . . . what you did to Sihon and Og, the two kings of the Amorites whom you completely destroyed. When we heard of it, our hearts melted and everyone's courage failed because of you . . ." (Joshua 2:9-11).

That's the way the nations that lived around the Incans felt.

Questions
- What was the goal of the Incan Empire?
- According to Matthew 28:19-20, what goal has God given us?

Warriors

Warfare

I f the Incans did go to war with another nation, they fought with bows and arrows, spears, darts, short swords, battle axes, and slings. They made their spear tips and arrow tips out of bone or copper.

The High Inca's weapons were tipped with gold and silver. Gold and silver are very soft metals, so they make terrible weapons. But the Incans felt they were the only metals fit for the weapons of their god, the king.

Because the Incans had good roads and a good communication system, the High Inca could gather the army together quickly. He himself usually led the army into battle.

The army marched quickly to the place where they would fight. Along the way they would stop at the storage buildings to rest and to gather supplies. As we have already seen, these buildings had a good supply of grain, weapons, and anything else the army might need.

The Incan army was very strong. Yet they were eventually defeated by the Spaniards. When the Spaniards took over the Incan Empire, they helped themselves to the supplies in the storage buildings. The buildings were so full that the Spaniards lived off the supplies for months!

Questions

- How were the High Inca's weapons different from the weapons of all the other Incan fighting men?
- How did the Incans' roads and communication system help the Incans to fight?

✹☺✹☺✹☺✹☺✹☺✹☺✹☺✹☺✹

A Different Way of Fighting

The Incans tried to fight more by words and wisdom than by violence. They tried to convince other nations to become Incans. Even if they did eventually go to war with another nation, the High Inca was always willing to stop fighting if the two sides could come to some agreement. He did not think it was necessary to completely destroy his enemies.

Sometimes the Incan army would destroy the crops of the other nation so that their enemies would not have enough food to eat. If the people of the other nation were starving, they might be more willing to become Incans.

However, the Incan soldiers were not allowed to take food for themselves. Soldiers were not allowed to take anything from their enemies to use for themselves. The Incans believed that even battles belonged to the High Inca and to the Sun.

If the enemies did not want to become Incans, even after the Incans declared war, the Incans showed no mercy. They would fight hard. And most of the time, they would win.

Question

• How did the Incans fight "more by wisdom and words than by violence"?

☀☺☀☺☀☺☀☺☀☺☀☺☀☺☀☺☀

Victory

What happened when the Incans defeated an enemy?

What Defeat Meant to Other Nations

First, the Incans erected temples in the conquered nation. They brought priests to live in the conquered nation so the people there could worship the Sun. The Incans allowed the people of the conquered nation to continue worshiping their own gods, but they had to worship the Sun more. They had to agree that the Sun was greater than their gods.

The Incans usually brought to Cuzco any idols that the people had used to worship their own gods. They placed these idols in a temple reserved for lesser gods.

The second thing the Incans did when they conquered another nation was to change the way the people lived, so they would become like the Incans.

First, the Incans counted the people of the other nation and saw how much land they had. Then they divided the land into three parts: one part for the Sun, one part for the High Inca, and one part for the people.

The Incans did whatever they could to give the people of the conquered nation the same benefits that the Incans enjoyed. If the people did the work they were told to do, they would always have enough food to eat.

To make sure everyone would have enough food, the High Inca sent men into the conquered nation to help them develop new fields for crops. They would help build canals to bring water to the fields. They would help dig terraces on the sides of mountains. They did all this so that more crops could be produced.

While the land and people were being blessed in this way, the High Inca brought the leaders of the conquered nation and their families to the city of Cuzco. These people became Curacas. In Cuzco, the Incans would teach the Curacas the language, manners, and customs of the Incan people. They would also teach the Curacas about Incan government.

When the Incans had finished teaching the Curacas all about the way they should live, the High Inca gave them gifts. Then he sent most of them home. All the Curacas who were oldest sons he kept to stay in Cuzco. These oldest sons had to live near the High Inca and become part of his court.

The High Inca wanted the people of the conquered nation to be faithful to him and serve him. If the oldest sons in the conquered nation were living close to the High Inca, and serving him every day, then the rest of the people of that nation would be more likely to serve the High Inca, too.

Questions
- What did an Incan victory mean to the people who were defeated by the Incans?
- After the Incans defeated a nation, how did they help the people of that nation?
- Why do you think the High Inca wanted the oldest sons of the Curacas to live close to him and serve him? How would this cause the rest of the people of that nation to be faithful to the High Inca?

🌞☺🌞☺🌞☺🌞☺🌞☺🌞☺🌞☺🌞☺🌞

What Victory Meant to the Incans
To the High Inca and his army, a victory meant a great parade in Cuzco.

The Bible tells us that "when [Jesus] ascended on high, he led captives in his train and gave gifts to men." In other words, Jesus led a parade. He was in front, and the captives were behind (Ephesians 4:8).

The Bible also says that "God . . . always leads us in triumphal procession in Christ and through us spreads everywhere the fragrance of the knowledge of him" (2 Corinthians 2:14).

The processions described in these verses are like the kind of parades that the Incans enjoyed after they won a war.

At the head of the Incan parade, the nobles carried the High Inca on a golden chair on his litter. The nobles carried the High Inca under the arches of triumph to the temple of the Sun.

The whole army marched behind the High Inca. The soldiers carried the goods that the army had taken from their enemies. At the end of the parade, behind the army, came the chiefs of the conquered nations (the Curacas).

All the people of Cuzco came out for the parade. They dressed in their brightest clothing. You could tell which province a person was from by the clothes he or she wore.

The people waved banners and branches, and threw fragrant flowers in the path of the High Inca and the army. As the High Inca and the army marched over the flowers, the flowers would be crushed under their feet and the fragrance went up into the air. The whole celebration was bright, cheerful, noisy, and extremely fragrant!

The nobles brought the High Inca to the temple of the Sun. Once they arrived at the temple, the nobles would take the High Inca's royal robes off him. They would take off his headdress, his jewels, and everything else that made him look different from the ordinary people of Tavantinsuyu.

The High Inca would then take off his own shoes and go inside the temple. There he stretched himself face-down on the ground before the Sun, and thanked the Sun for his victory.

The Incans believed that all glory came *from* the Sun, and all glory had to return back *to* the Sun.

The Bible says that all things are from Yahweh, and through Yahweh and to Yahweh—not the Sun! "For from him and through him and to him are all things. To *him* be the glory forever!" (Romans 11:36; emphasis added.)

The Bible tells us there will come a time when Jesus, the true Prophet, Priest, and King, will "[hand] over the kingdom to God the

Father after he has destroyed all dominion, authority, and power. For he must reign until he has put all his enemies under his feet" (I Corinthians 15:24-25).

Yahweh has highly exalted Jesus, and given "him the name which is above every name, that at the name of Jesus every knee should bow, of those who are in heaven, and on earth, and under the earth, and that every tongue should confess that Jesus Christ is Lord, to the glory of God the Father" (Philippians 2:9-11).

Questions
• What did an Incan victory mean to the Incans?
• The Bible says that Christians are soldiers in Jesus' army. "The weapons we fight with are not the weapons of the world" (2 Corinthians 10:3-5), but Jesus is going to use his army to destroy "all dominion, authority and power" (1 Corinthians 15:24). "The gates of Hades will not overcome [the Church]" (Matthew 16:18). What do you think will be the results of Jesus' victory in the lives of the people whom He defeats? What will be the results of this victory for Jesus and His people?

☀☺☀☺☀☺☀☺☀☺☀☺☀☺☀☺☀

Religion

The Incans believed that their laws had been given by the Sun. They believed that, by obeying the laws, they were honoring the Sun and worshiping him.

When they went to war, the reason they fought was to spread their religion to other nations so those nations, too, would worship the Sun. So even their wars were religious.

Everything the Incan people did was for the Sun and for his servant, the High Inca.

Beliefs

Gods of the Incans

The Incans' "greatest" god was the Sun. But more than that, they believed the Sun rules history because the Sun gives light and warmth to the earth, and gives life to vegetables. If it were not for the Sun, no one could live.

The Incans also believed that the Sun was the father of the Incan royal family—the High Incas and the other Incas who helped rule the country. They believed it was the Sun who started the Incan Empire.

Because the Incans believed the Sun was so great, they built temples for the Sun in every Incan city and almost every village.

In the Incan religion, there were also other gods that were not as great as the Sun. There were the Moon, the Stars, the planet Venus, Thunder and Lightning. The Moon was the Sun's sister, but also his wife. The Stars were the Moon's royal court. Venus was the Sun's messenger boy. Thunder and Lightning were the ministers of the Sun.

Sacred Valley of the Inca

All these were considered lesser gods. The Incans also believed that the Rainbow showed the glory of these lesser gods.

Below the lesser gods there were little gods and goddesses: the Wind, the Earth, the Air, Copper, Tin, Gold, and others. The Incans even believed that some of the great mountains and rivers were gods and goddesses.

There was one more god that a very small number of Incans worshiped. This god was called *Pachacamac* (puh-CHAW-kuh-muck). Those who worshiped Pachacamac believed that he was even greater than the Sun. They believed that he was invisible, that he was the creator of the universe, and that he ruled over everything.

The problem was Pachacamac could not be seen. Most Incans refused to worship him because, they said, "At least you can see the Sun, the Moon, the High Inca and all the other gods. What good is a god if you can't see him (or it)?"

So Pachacamac was the Incans' "unknown god" (see Acts 17:23). There was only one temple for Pachacamac. It was in a valley close to where the city of Lima, Peru is today.

Although the Incans believed in many gods, they only believed in one evil spirit. His name was *Cupay* (COO-pie). But the Incans didn't believe that Cupay had much power. So no one was afraid of him. And no one offered him any sacrifices.

Questions
• Who was *Pachacamac*?
• Who was *Cupay*?
• Why weren't the Incans afraid of Cupay?

🌟 ☺ 🌟 ☺ 🌟 ☺ 🌟 ☺ 🌟 ☺ 🌟 ☺ 🌟 ☺ 🌟 ☺ 🌟

People's Souls
The Incans believed that people's souls continue to live even after their bodies die. If the person who died had been bad in this life, then he would go to the center of the earth. There he would have to work hard forever and ever.

If the person who died had been good in this life, then he would enjoy a wonderful life in eternity. He would have many nice things, and he would not have to do any work. Everyone else would serve him.

The Incans also believed that people's souls would one day return to their bodies and make the bodies live again.

In order to help make this happen, the Incans preserved the bodies of those who died. They would put the body out in the cold, dry air, high up in the mountains. They would leave it there until it dried out. After being dried out in this way, it would take a very long time for a body to decompose.

Question

- The word *compose* means to make something by putting things together in an orderly way. What does *decompose* mean?

☀ ☺ ☀ ☺ ☀ ☺ ☀ ☺ ☀ ☺ ☀ ☺ ☀ ☺ ☀ ☺ ☀

Practices
Festivals

The Incans had four main festivals. All of them were related to the Sun.

They had a festival for the first day of summer, called the *summer solstice*. This is when the Sun is at its highest point in the sky. They had a festival for the first day of winter, called the *winter solstice*. This is when the Sun is at its lowest point in the sky.

They had a festival for the first day of spring, called the *vernal* or *spring equinox*. This is when daytime and nighttime are equal. And they had a festival for the first day of fall, called the *autumnal* or *fall equinox*. This is when daytime and nighttime are equal again.[h]

The Greatest Festival: Raymi

The Incans' greatest festival was the one that occurred on the first day of summer. They thought that the Sun was "strongest" when it was at its highest point in the sky. So they had their greatest festival on the day when they thought their chief god, the Sun, was greatest. This festival was called the Feast of Raymi.

For three days before Raymi, everyone fasted. No one was permitted to eat, and no one was allowed to have a fire in his home.

On the day of the festival, everyone got up early to greet the Sun as it came up. The people dressed in their brightest, most joyful clothes. The nobles wore special jewelry. The people celebrated Raymi much like they celebrated a victory in battle.

As soon as the Sun's rays hit the highest building, all the Incans shouted as loudly as they could. They sang loud songs of triumph and played their instruments loudly. This was the way they worshiped the Sun on its greatest day.

The High Inca poured liquor out of a huge golden vase as an offering to the Sun. Then he led the people as they all went to the great Temple of the Sun at Cuzco.

When the High Inca reached the temple, he went in and worshiped the Sun by himself. Then he came back out and prepared a llama to sacrifice to the Sun.

After the High Inca killed the llama, a priest took its kidneys out and used them to try to foretell the future. If the future looked "bad," the priests would slaughter another llama, and try to foretell the future again. They hoped that what they foretold about the future would be good instead of bad.

51

After the priests tried to foretell the future, they started a fire. They used a mirror to reflect the Sun's rays on a piece of dried cotton. If the sky was too cloudy for the mirror to work, the priests would rub sticks together until they were hot enough that they would burn.

The Incans believed that if the sky was too cloudy for the mirror to work, then something bad might happen in the future.

Trying to foretell the future is called divination. Yahweh clearly tells us in the Bible (Deuteronomy 18:10-14) that He hates divination, and that people should not practice it.

After the priests had started a strong fire, they burned the llama that they had sacrificed. Then they passed on some of the fire to a group of women called Virgins of the Sun.

These women passed the fire to all the Incan people, so they could take it home with them and relight the fires in their homes. Then all the homes in the whole Incan Empire would have some of the fire from the Feast of Raymi.

But before the people went back to their homes, they ate a big banquet. Many llamas were slaughtered. The High Inca, and all the people in his court, and all the people at the festival enjoyed the great feast.

Questions

- What was the chief god of the Incans?
- Please define *solstice*.
- Please define *equinox*.
- Why do you think the two solstices and the two equinoxes were the days the Incans chose for their biggest festivals?
- What was *Raymi*?
- What happened during Raymi?

Sacrifices

Sacrifices were very important in the Incan religion. By offering sacrifices to the Sun, they were worshiping the Sun. The Incans usually sacrificed animals, and parts of plants, like grain, flowers, and sweet-smelling gums. But sometimes they sacrificed people. They killed people in order to give them as an offering to the Sun.[i]

When the Incans sacrificed a person, it was usually in honor of some great event: the crowning of a new High Inca, the birth of the Coya's first son, or some great victory.

Although the Incans did not sacrifice people as much as other peoples did, it was still wrong to do it at all. Yahweh hates this kind of practice (Deuteronomy 12:31).

Temples

A temple *building* was very important to the Incans like it was to the Jews in the Old Testament.

But there were two big differences. The Jews worshiped Yahweh; the Incans did not know Him. The Jews only had one temple; the Incans had many. The Incans had three or four hundred temples in the city of Cuzco, plus hundreds of other temples spread throughout the empire.

Coricancha

For the Incans, the most important temple was called *Coricancha*, which means "the Place of Gold." It was the main temple of the Sun.

This temple had a huge golden image of the Sun on one wall. The image was enhanced with emeralds and precious stones.

To the Incans, gold was the "tears of the Sun," so Coricancha and all other temples to the Sun were filled with gold. There was even a broad belt of gold that went around the outside of Coricancha. This temple was the only Incan building that had any kind of decoration on the outside.

Other temples were a part of Coricancha. So besides being the main temple to the Sun, Coricancha also included other smaller temples. Among them: a temple to the Moon, one to the Stars, one to Thunder and Lightning, and one to the Rainbow.

The temple to the Moon was almost like the main temple to the Sun. The biggest difference was that the Moon temple was filled with silver instead of gold.

Everything in all of these temples was made of gold or silver. There were gold and silver ornaments, utensils, vases, instruments used for worship, underground water pipes, . . . and even gold and silver garden tools!

Question

• Describe *Coricancha*.

Priests and Religious Workers
The High Priests

The High Inca was the Incans' chief priest and worship leader. There was another priest called the High Priest. He was not as great as the High Inca, but he was greater than everyone else in Incan society.

The High Inca chose the person who would be High Priest. Once he was chosen, this man would be the High Priest for the rest of his life. Usually the High Priest was a brother or another close relative of the High Inca.

Other Priests

Besides the High Inca and the High Priest, there were other priests, too. They served in the temples.[j]

The Incan priests were different from the Jewish priests in the Old Testament. The Jewish priests were also teachers (Deuteronomy 31:9-13). The Incan priests weren't. The Jewish priests had contact

---

Note For Adults:[j]

Until Jesus came, Yahweh had always taught that there was a particular place for us to worship. In Deuteronomy 12:2-3, He said, "You are to seek the place [Yahweh] your God will choose from among all your tribes to put his Name there for his dwelling. To that place you must go [when you] bring your burnt offerings and sacrifices, your tithes and special gifts."

When Jesus came, He taught His disciples that there would be a time when people would worship Yahweh "neither on this mountain nor in Jerusalem" (John 4:21). Worship would take place anywhere and at any time. What matters is not the place but the spirit and truth of the worship. In 1 Corinthians 6 we learn a little more about this issue of where worship takes place. According to 1 Corinthians 6, one of the reasons the specific location is not so important is because our *bodies* are temples of the Holy Spirit!

Ruins of the Temple of the Sun

with the common people. The Incan priests didn't. Ordinary citizens of the Incan Empire weren't allowed to see or speak to the priests.

And finally, of course, the Jewish priests served Yahweh. The Incan priests did not.

The Incans had a lot of priests—more than four thousand just at Coricancha! The priests at Coricancha were men from the royal family. In other areas of the country, the Curacas served as priests.

Virgins of the Sun

The Virgins of the Sun were young women who had been dedicated to the service of the Sun. When they were very young, these girls were taken from their homes and put in convents where they were taught how to serve the Sun.

The Virgins of the Sun spun thread and embroidered fabric for the temples. They also made clothes for the High Inca and his family.

But their most important job was to watch over the sacred fire to keep it going until the next Raymi. If the Virgins accidentally let the fire go out, the Incans believed something very bad would happen. Maybe the High Inca would die, or the Incan army might lose a battle.

When the Virgins of the Sun were old enough to be married, the most beautiful ones became wives of the High Inca. The High Inca could have as many as several thousand wives!

Questions

- We have read very much about the Incans' way of life. Discuss what you think is good and bad about their culture.
- What things do you think people today might learn from them?
- What things should people avoid today? Why?

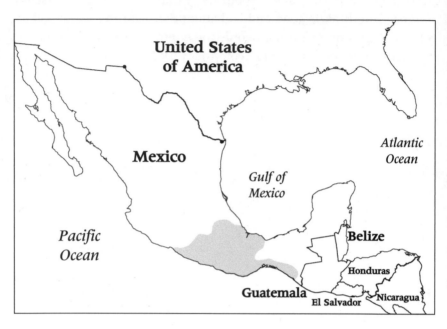

Aztec Territory in Southern Mexico

Aztecs

A Spaniard named Hernán Cortés[1] came to Central America in 1519. Along with him came many Spanish soldiers.

Soon after they arrived, there was a terrible battle between the Spaniards and the Indians of Tabasco. About 40,000 Indian warriors attacked the Spaniards. There were only 580 Spaniards, but they fought very well. The Spaniards killed more than 800 Indians, but the Indians only killed two Spaniards.

Cortés and his men had contact with other Indian tribes in the next few months. One of these tribes was the Aztecs.

A group of Aztecs came to visit Cortés while he was still staying on

Cortés' men fired a gun, causing panic among their Indian visitors who dove into the sea from fear. Drawing from the *Codex Florentino.*

the east coast of Central America. The Aztecs were dressed in jaguar skins. They came in peace.

When the Aztecs met Cortés, they fell to their knees and kissed the ground in front of his feet.

Then they dressed him in clothes fit for a king. They gave him golden jewelry. They gave him a headdress made from beautiful red, white, and yellowish green *quetzal* (KET-sul) feathers. They gave him a crown made from jaguar skin. And they gave him a shield covered with gold and pearls.

After Cortés received all this honor, he pretended to be angry. It seemed that the Indians were treating him like a god, so he thought

---

[1] Cortes is also sometimes spelled Cortez.

he would try to get even more gifts from them. He pretended he was a god, and acted as if he was angry because the Indians' offerings were too small.

"Is this all?" he shouted. "Is this the way you greet your guests?"

Cortés commanded his men to fire a cannon. The cannon roared with a sound louder than anything the Indians had ever heard. Lots

Quetzal bird

of smoke came out, and the thing smelled awful. Moments later, a tree several hundred yards away exploded.

The Indians collapsed in fright.

Later, Cortés and his men were very surprised to see four thousand Aztec warriors suddenly come into their camp.

Happily for the Spaniards, none of the Aztec warriors carried weapons.

"We have come," said the Indians, "not to make war, but to offer gifts."

Before they left, the Indian warriors gave the Spaniards great treasures. There was a helmet filled with gold dust. And there were golden figurines of animals, plants, and seashells. The biggest gifts of all were two big disks—one made of gold and the other of silver. Each disk was as big around as the wheel of a cart, and as thick as a man's hand is wide. The gifts were far greater than anything the Spaniards could have imagined.

Can these things really be? the Spaniards wondered. *Can there really be so much gold in this land? Have we discovered the source of all riches?*

But these were not the only questions in the minds of the Spaniards. Before the Aztecs presented the treasures, they did something that made the Spaniards ask other questions—at least in their minds. And these other questions were very disturbing. *What kind of people were these Aztecs anyway?*

When the Aztecs first came into the Spaniards' camp, they told the Spaniards that they had prepared a banquet. They wanted the Spaniards to enjoy their hospitality. The Spaniards weren't sure what to expect, but they accepted the invitation.

The Aztec warriors spread out a big feast for Cortés and his men. There were turkeys, eggs, fruits, and breads. They asked the Spaniards to sit down.

The meal looked good. The Spaniards had been eating stale biscuits and salt beef for a long time. So, as they saw the food spread out before them, they smacked their lips in anticipation.

Then, just as the Spaniards sat down, a group of Aztec priests grabbed an Indian. The priests threw the man to the ground and killed him. Then they sprinkled his blood on the food.[2]

It was disgusting! It was horrible! The Spaniards didn't know what to do. They coughed and spat and rolled their eyes. Why? they wondered. *Why did these Indians do this? But they had no answers.*

Questions

Cortés and his men said that they came to America in order to represent the God of the Bible. We will learn more about this later. But for now, think about these questions:

- When Cortés first met the Aztecs, how did he fail to honor Yahweh?
- How do you think Yahweh feels about this? (See Acts 12:21-23.)
- Read Acts 14:8-23. What did Paul and Barnabas do when people thought they were gods?

� decorative dingbats 🌞☺🌞☺🌞☺🌞☺🌞☺🌞☺🌞☺🌞

Religion

The Aztecs were very religious. Religion was the most important part of their lives. But their religion seems strange to those of us who follow the Lord Jesus Christ. It seems strange because the Aztecs' religion was demonic.

Warwick Bray, author of *Everyday Life of the Aztecs,* wrote: "Religion was the [main motivation behind everything in Aztec society, from] sports, games and war [to] commerce [and] politics. . . . It

---

[2] The priests threw the Indian on his back and cut out his heart. Then they took the heart and sprinkled blood all over the food. This type of practice will be explained more later.

[played a part] in every act of the individual, from birth until the moment when the priests cremated his [body] and [buried] the ashes."

Indeed, their religion played a part in their lives even after their ashes were buried. It determined where they would spend eternity. Religion is more than bowing down before some-

Aztec priests in ceremonial headdress.

thing or someone. It is people giving themselves to something or someone. It is people on the way to eternal life or eternal death.

Beliefs
Gods: The "Four Hundred Rabbits"

The Aztecs had very strong beliefs about their gods. But there were so many gods, and the beliefs were confusing. Scholars today can't tell us in detail what the Aztecs believed. But we do know some things.

The Aztecs believed that different gods had power over different areas of life. For instance, there were gods for food and gods for water. There were gods for wealth, gods for health, gods for having children . . . gods for almost everything. There were also different gods for different places.[3]

All of the Aztecs' hundreds of gods, together, were called the Four Hundred Rabbits.

While the Aztecs believed in hundreds of gods, there were three or four gods whom they respected more than the others.

---

[3] The Aztecs' beliefs were similar to what we read in the Old Testament concerning the Moabites (Numbers 23:13, 27) and the Arameans (I Kings 20:28). The Moabites and Arameans believed that there were different gods for different places.

Moyocoyani

A few Aztecs believed that there was really only one god, even though it seemed like there were many gods. They thought this one god just appeared different at different times and in different places. They called this god *Moyocoyani* (moy-oh-coy-AW-nee), which means "He Who Gives Existence to Himself."[a]

Note For Adults:[a]

Look up Exodus 3:14. Moyocoyani would be a good Nahuatl (Aztec language) translation for the Hebrew words "I AM THAT I AM" or "I AM WHO I AM"—words directly related to Yahweh's name. In Romans 1:18-23, Yahweh tells us that people "suppress the truth [about God] . . . since what may be known about God is plain to them, because God has made it plain to them. . . . [But] although they knew God, they neither glorified him as God nor gave thanks to him, but their thinking became futile and their foolish hearts were darkened. Although they claimed to be wise, they became fools and exchanged the glory of . . . God for images made to look like mortal man and birds and animals and reptiles." As we read about Moyocoyani and the other gods of the Aztecs, you will see how true this is.

Those Aztecs who believed in Moyocoyani said he (or, more accurately, "it" (Moyocoyani was neither male nor female)) was invisible, all-powerful, and present everywhere throughout the universe. Another name for Moyocoyani was *Tloque Nahuaque* (tloh-kway nah-WHAH-kway), "Lord of Everywhere."

Moyocoyani was very different from Yahweh, the God of the Bible, whom we worship. Yahweh is invisible, all-powerful, and present everywhere. But Yahweh is also a person. He is our heavenly father (Matthew 5:16, 45, 48; 6:4ff; etc.); He is also our heavenly husband-to-be (Isaiah 54; Ezekiel 16; Hosea 2; Revelation 21). Most of all, He wants us to come to know

(cont. on next pg.)

Him. In fact, He says, many of the things that happen in our world He makes to happen so that we will come to know Him (see, for example, Exodus 6:7; 7:17; 8:22; 11:7; 16:12; 1 Kings 20:28; Isaiah 49:23; etc.!).

Yahweh teaches us that we are to make no idols of or for Him (Exodus 20:4-5). But that is not because He is unknowable (see Acts 17:22-31; Romans 1:18-19; Galatians 4:8-9; 1 John 2:13-14). He simply doesn't want us to become confused about who He is. He is not like anything He created. He is totally different from everything He created.

An Aztec ruler once built a temple for Moyocoyani, but, unlike every other temple built by the Aztecs, this one contained no idols.

While Moyocoyani was supposed to be all-powerful and present everywhere, you couldn't possibly get to know him (or "it"; Moyocoyani was not a person). To the Aztecs, Moyocoyani was the great unknown and unknowable god. That's why most people ignored him.

Huitzilopochtli

The great Sun god of the Aztecs was *Huitzilopochtli* (WEE-tseel-oh-POTCH-tlee). They believed Huitzilopochtli was the Sun.

According to the Aztecs, Huitzilopochtli was always fighting the forces of the night. He fought his brothers and sisters—the Moon and the Stars. According to the Aztecs, when these other gods were winning the fight, night came. And there was a time every day when the other gods were winning. Night kept coming every 24 hours.

The Aztecs believed that every time night came, Huitzilopochtli had been killed. And if the Sun was dead, it couldn't shine. So they were always afraid that there might not be another day.

The only way there could be another day was if Huitzilopochtli could be reborn. The only way their Sun god could be reborn was if he had enough strength. The only way he could get enough strength was if they gave him enough of the right kind of food.

Temple of Huitzilopochtli

And what was the best kind of food for the Sun? The human heart and human blood.

That is how the practice of sacrificing people became so important to the Aztecs. They thought that if they didn't sacrifice people, the Sun would never rise again.

Tlaloc

Huitzilopochtli was the most famous Aztec god. But the most powerful god was *Tlaloc* (TLAHL-ock). This was the rain god or "He Who Makes Things Grow."

The Aztecs believed that Tlaloc was usually friendly to humans. But, if he became angry, he would cause their crops to be destroyed. He would do this by sending floods or lightning, or by sending rain at a bad time. Rain might come during harvest time, so the people couldn't harvest the crops. Or rain might cause the crops to rot.

Xipe Totec

Finally, there was *Xipe Totec* (SHEE-pay TOE-teck), "Our Lord the Flayed One." He was the god of spring. He was also the favorite god of the goldsmiths—men who made things out of gold.

Xipe Totec's face and clothes were red. For clothing, he used skin that came from human beings. The human skin that Xipe Totec used for clothing stood for the flowers, grass, trees, and everything else that covers the earth.

Carving of Xipe Totec

Questions

- Describe *Moyocoyani, Huitzilopochtli, Tlaloc,* and *Xipe Totec.*
- What were the *Four Hundred Rabbits*?
- Do you think the Aztecs respected the Four Hundred Rabbits? Why or why not? (Is a rabbit something that is powerful? If you knew that the god you worshiped on a particular day was only one of hundreds of others who all fought each other, would you expect your prayers to be answered?)

Creation

According to the Bible, the world was created just once. According to the Aztecs, the world was created five times.

In each of the first four creations, one of four brother gods managed to become the Sun (the sun we see in the sky).

The problem was that whichever god became the Sun also became the chief god. The chief god had the right to rule everything and everyone else—including his brothers. And none of the other brothers liked that! They all wanted to be the chief god who could rule the others.

So the four brothers fought among themselves. And every time they fought, the one who had become the Sun was knocked out of the sky. When that happened, the earth was destroyed, and the people who lived on the earth at that time were also destroyed.

This happened four times. The earth was destroyed and then rebuilt. Finally, the fifth world was created. All the gods got together and agreed that only one god should become the Sun. But who would that be? They decided that it would be a god who was willing to sacrifice himself.

So a poor, humble god jumped into a fire. He was reborn as the Sun.

But now that they had the Sun in the sky, the gods had a new problem—the Sun never moved. It stood perfectly still. The other gods were very worried. What could they do?

Quetzalcoatl

They decided to throw themselves into the fire as well. Then at last the Sun began to move.

Now there was a world. There was a Sun in the sky. The Sun moved. But there were no people.

One of the gods, named *Quetzalcoatl* (KETsl-co-AHtl), figured he knew how to make human beings.

He went to the underworld to get the bones of all the people who had been made in the previous worlds.

On his way back from the underworld, Quetzalcoatl slipped and fell. When he fell, he dropped all the bones. And when he dropped them, the bones shattered.

Quetzalcoatl couldn't figure out how to put the bones back together again. So he took some of his own blood and sprinkled it over the broken pieces.

The pieces of bone that Quetzalcoatl used were all different shapes and sizes. That's why people come in so many different shapes and sizes.That's how people were made—according to the Aztecs.

Questions

- Describe how the world and people were made, according to the Aztecs.
- How is the story that the Aztecs told similar to what we read in the Bible?
- How is it different from what the Bible tells us?

☀☺☀☺☀☺☀☺☀☺☀☺☀☺☀☺☀

Other Beliefs

The Aztecs had many superstitions, and they lived by them.

When a child's tooth fell out, the mother would toss it down a mouse hole. The Aztecs believed that if she didn't do this, a new tooth would not grow in.

Aztec children tried not to lean against square pillars. That was because they didn't want to grow up to be liars.

The Aztecs believed that comets and earthquakes were signs of especially bad things to come.[4]

By the way: The Bible says that there is no such thing as "luck." Yahweh, our God, controls all things that happen. The things that He brings into our lives may seem pleasant or unpleasant. But they are not the result of "good" or "bad" "luck." (See Exodus 7:3; 9:16;

---

[4] We'll find out about the historical significance of this superstition in just a few days!

10:1,2; Proverbs 16:9; 21:1; John 6:37,44; Acts 4:27-28; Ephesians 1:4; Colossians 1:16-17.)

The Aztecs believed that at night ghosts and demons could be found everywhere.

Question

• What do you think about the common expression, "Good luck"? Do you think Christians should use this phrase? If not, what do you think we could say instead?

🌞😊🌞😊 🌞😊🌞😊🌞😊🌞 😊 🌞😊🌞😊🌞

Practices

Sacrifices[5,b]

Sometimes people describe the greatness of the Aztec civilization without describing the bad parts of it. It would be wrong to say the Aztec civilization was all good, because it certainly wasn't.

The gods of the Aztecs were actually demons. And demons want to ruin the lives of human beings. Because the Aztecs' gods were evil, the religious practices of the Aztecs were also evil.

The Aztecs believed that the gods had sacrificed themselves at the creation of the world. They believed that this meant human beings should sacrifice themselves to feed the Sun and all the other gods.

Pyramid of Quetzalcoatl

---

[5] Before you proceed, you may want to pre-read the description as well as the note *b* on page 70.

Note For Adults:[b]

Some readers have become angry or upset when they have read this passage. They have expressed themselves as being angry at the author because he included information about the Aztec sacrifices. I wonder, however, if such anger is not misplaced. Should not anger be directed against the Aztec system of sacrifice? Or, far more, at our world's wretched condition, the result of human wickedness and sin?

Let us put the Aztecs' sacrifices in context. Sacrifice—even human sacrifice—was not, and is not, unique to the Aztecs. Even our own Christian faith is based on a blood sacrifice, a human blood sacrifice, the sacrifice of the God-man Jesus Christ.

By saying this, I do not in any way wish to denigrate the sacrifice of our Lord by comparing it to the vile sacrifices of the Aztecs. What I want to do is point out that revulsion at descriptions of blood sacrifice, revulsion, even, at the description of human blood sacrifice, may have less to do with the description of the sacrifice than it has to do with the vile nature of sacrifices to demonic "gods." Thus it seems to me that we should be more angry at those who do the awful things than at the person who describes them—just as the U.S. government should be more angry at the practice of abortion than at the abortion protesters who display photographs of aborted babies or who present pro-abortion presidential candidates with jars containing the remains of aborted babies.

Historian Otto Scott has pointed out that many scholars admire the so-called *Grandeur that was Rome and the Glory that was Greece*. This view of history, he claims, is just as "politically-correct" as the view of Aztec civilization that admires their "architecture, skills, labor system and agriculture" while ignoring their grisly system of sacrifice.

Our common, politically-correct view of Rome and Greece as "grand" and "glorious" ignores the fact that both civilizations were "based on slavery, used torture as an instrument of the courts, and human sacrifice as part of religion and politics."

Euripides described the Greek sacrifice of Iphegenia; Herodotus described human sacrifices in Egypt; Plato spoke of human sacrifices as 'a common custom.' In Rome sacrifices 'for magical purposes' were outlawed from 95 B.C., but human sacrifices for religious and political reasons were conducted in public for as long as Rome was pagan.

In 63 B.C. Cataline and his accomplices sacrificed a boy and ate his . . . flesh. . . . Julius Caesar sacrificed mutineers in the name of Mars; Augustus, Nero, Caligula, Commodus, Marcus Aurelius—indeed, all the Roman emperors until Constantine—ordered human sacrifices.

Julian the Apostate . . . "filled his palace at Antioch with the corpses of human victims. . . . After his death [A.D. 361] the body of a woman was found hanging by her hair in a temple at Carrae. [Julian] had inspected her entrails to divine the issue of his [final military] campaign."

Rhadagaisus, a Saxon leader, sacrificed a Roman Christian every day—and continued to do this at the time of Charlemagne, who died in 842 A.D. The Franks practiced human sacrifice long after Clovis, who died in 511 A.D. The Germans abandoned the worship of Odin slowly and reluctantly over a long period. The Scandinavians sacrificed humans to the god of battle, to avert drought, and as a religious rite till the middle of the eleventh century.

—Otto Scott, *The Great Christian Revolution* (Vallecito, CA: Russ House Books, 1991), pp. 83-84.

Should we "sanitize" our history so our children know as little as possible of the true reasons Jesus came to die? I believe not.

Rather than directing anger against the present author for including a description of the Aztecs' blood sacrifices, perhaps you and your child[ren] can pray a prayer of confession and repentance for "the sin that so easily entangles," asking God to permit you to "run with perseverance the race marked out for [you]" (Hebrews 12:1).

In the middle of *Tenochtitlan* (teh-NOTCH-tit-lahn), the Aztecs' capital city, the Aztecs built a big pyramid. It was 90 feet high and had steps leading to the top. At the top of this pyramid they built two temples. One was for Huitzilopochtli, and the other for Tlaloc.

In front of these two temples were two big, round-topped stones, about knee-high. They were altars designed for sacrificing people.

The person who was about to be sacrificed would walk up the steps to the top of the pyramid. Then four priests would grab him and throw him down on his back on top of the altar. They would hold him there while another priest cut out his heart. They would throw the body down the steps of the pyramid. Then they would offer the heart and blood to Huitzilopochtli.

Most of us would think that a person would not want to be sacrificed. He would not want to die. But it seems, most of the people whom the Aztecs sacrificed were happy to die. They believed they were doing a great and good deed. They believed they were feeding the gods.

The Aztecs finished building the Great Pyramid at Tenochtitlan in 1487. This was only forty-two years before the Spaniards came. When the temple was dedicated, the priests sacrificed somewhere between 20,000 and 50,000 people!

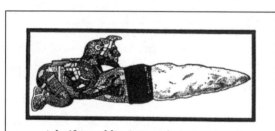

A knife used by Aztec priests to cut out the hearts of sacrificial victims. The entire handle is inlaid with turquoise, mother-of-pearl, and malachite.

The captives stood in four lines waiting to be sacrificed. Each line was about two miles long. It took four days and three nights for the priests to sacrifice all those people.

As far as we know, that was the largest sacrifice. But after that, the Aztecs continued to sacrifice many people each year. People who have studied the Aztecs say that between 10,000 and 50,000 people were sacrificed each year. That means, if the sacrifices were only done during daylight hours, the Aztecs would have had to kill at least one person every half hour, or maybe even one person every five minutes. And this went on every hour of every day, throughout the year!

A Spaniard named Andres de Tapia, who came to Tenochtitlan in 1521, said he found many skulls that the Aztecs had collected. There were 136,000 of them. And that was not counting the skulls that the Aztecs had cemented together to build a tower.[c]

Most of the Aztecs' sacrifices for Huitzilopochtli were men who had been captured in war. But they sacrificed slaves and children as well.

Besides sacrifices to Huitzilpochtli, in the first and third months of every year the Aztecs used little children as sacrifices to Tlaloc. As we have already read, Tlaloc was the god of rain. The Aztecs believed that the more tears the children cried, the more rain would come in the next year. So they did everything possible to make the children cry as much as possible before they died.

In the sixth month of the year there was a great festival to Tlaloc. During the festival, anyone who had committed a major crime was thrown into a lake to drown.[6]

Note For Adults:[c]

Depending on how far you want to get into the subject, you may want to discuss some of the following points with your child(ren). Notice that the Aztecs' sacrifices had nothing to do with atonement. The Bible says, "The wages of sin is death." The blood sacrifice of Jesus—human sacrifice, but God's human sacrifice!—was necessary to pay the penalty of our (human) moral or ethical failure. It was designed to cover, pay for, or atone for, our sins. Aztec sacrifice—as pagan sacrifices in general—included no thought of sin, morality, or ethics. It was wholly functional. It was designed to give Huitzilopochtli good "food." Notice, too, that there was no hope in the Aztecs' sacrifices. The sacrifices had to keep on going forever. God's people in the Bible, even at the very beginning, looked forward to "Him who was to come" who would offer Himself as a once-for-all sacrifice for sin (Genesis 3:15; 49:10).

---

[6] The high point of the festival occurred when people who had been captured during the previous year were killed, their hearts cut out of their bodies and loaded into a canoe, and the canoe, together with all the hearts, pushed into the middle of the lake and sunk. Again, notice that there is no sense of atonement or propitiation for sins. It was just that certain classes of people seemed to make better or more appropriate meals for Tlaloc at different times of the year.

The sacrifices to *Xipe Totec* (SHEE-pay TOE-teck) were so horrible, we will not discuss them. Their purpose was to make the earth fruitful.[d]

Questions

- What was *Tenochtitlan*?
- How and why were the sacrifices that the Aztecs made different from the sacrifices that Yahweh calls us to make in the Bible?

🌞☺🌞☺🌞☺🌞☺🌞☺🌞☺🌞☺🌞☺🌞

History
The Lake of the Moon Before the Aztecs

Even before Jesus came to earth, people lived in the Valley of Mexico. They lived near the shores of the Lake of the Moon.

The Lake of the Moon was very shallow. The deepest part was only about nine to twelve feet deep. Yet the lake covered almost 400 square miles. At night, this huge, shallow lake made a wonderful mirror for the moon. That's how it got the name "Lake of the Moon."

The Lake of the Moon was actually made up of five smaller lakes. The largest of the five was *Lake Texcoco* (tesh-CAH-co).

There were many cities along the edges of the lake. Each city had its own ruler, so they were called city-states. All of them distrusted one another, and so they often fought each other.

After a war, the losers would have to pay *tribute* to the winners. This tribute was kind of like taxes, but it was different from the taxes we pay today. Instead of paying a certain amount of money, the losers would give the winners things that were valuable. It could be gold. It could be maize or wool. It could even be slaves. Basically, tribute was whatever the winners wanted the losers to give them.

"As long as you pay us," the winners would say, "we won't bother you. And as long as you keep paying us tribute, we will defend you against attack by anyone else."

Note For Adults:[d]

People who believe they need to sacrifice other people are in bondage to demons. The demons want to destroy people (John 10:10a). They want to destroy the lives of people here on earth. And they want to destroy people for eternity. They want people to experience eternal death.

Jesus said, "I came that they might have life, and might have it abundantly" (John 10:10b).

Jesus gave His own life to set us free from bondage. He died and rose again so that we could live forever with Him. But Yahweh does ask us to make sacrifices.

Yahweh wants us to be *living* sacrifices: ". . . [P]resent your bodies a living and holy sacrifice, acceptable to God, which is your spiritual service of worship" (Romans 12:1).

The kinds of hearts that Yahweh delights in are broken ones—hearts that repent of sin and turn to Him. "The sacrifices of God are a broken spirit; a broken and a contrite heart, O God, Thou wilt not despise" (Psalm 51:17).

"Through Him then, let us continually offer up a sacrifice of praise to God, that is the fruit of lips that give thanks to His name. And do not neglect doing good and sharing; for with such sacrifices God is pleased" (Hebrews 13:15-16).

The Aztecs were not the only people group that needed to be set free from the bondage of human sacrifice. In different places and at different times there have been other people groups who have practiced human sacrifice. People in Greece, people in Rome and other parts of Europe . . . and other parts of the world have been guilty of this terrible practice.

Even today, in America and many other parts of the world, babies are being killed inside their mothers' wombs. Who would want this to happen? Certainly *not Yahweh!*

The last group to enter the Valley of the Lake of the Moon were the *Mexica* (meh-SHEE-ca). "Mexico" comes from the name Mexica. The Mexica were the people we know as the Aztecs.

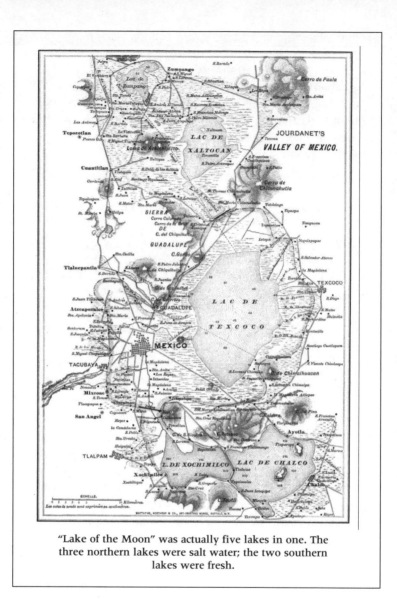

"Lake of the Moon" was actually five lakes in one. The three northern lakes were salt water; the two southern lakes were fresh.

1168-1325: The Years of Wandering

According to legends, in the year 1168, Huitzilopochtli told a group of people—the people we know today as Aztecs—to move south to a better homeland. The Aztecs didn't know where this better homeland was, but they set out to find it.

76

One day, we are told, they found an idol of Huitzilopochtli in a cave. Someone said that the idol would lead them to the place where they should go. The Aztecs left the cave. They hoped that Huitzilopochtli would lead them to their new homeland.

At every place they stopped, the people worshiped Huitzilopochtli. They wandered around for many years, but they kept trusting Huitzilopochtli to bring them to their new home. Early each spring they would send some members of their group to find a good place to plant crops. The people that were sent out would plant the crops. Then when the crops were ready to harvest, they sent for the rest of the tribe to come and join them.

Eventually, the group found that they were on the shores of Lake Texcoco. This was the largest part of the Lake of the Moon (see map on page 76). By the time they arrived at the lake, there were maybe a few thousand people in the group. These people were the original Aztecs.

At first, the Aztecs were *squatters*. This meant they lived on whatever land they could find. It would be like someone coming into your backyard and setting up a tent there. You didn't give them permission to stay in your yard. But they "squat" and stay anyway.[7]

Usually squatters are forced to move on. The people who live in a place don't want a big group of people moving in to stay. So they tell them to leave. This is what usually happened to the Aztecs. The local peoples didn't like them very much.

At one stop, the local people gave the Aztecs a campsite on a rocky hillside. The hillside was full of rattlesnakes. A few days after the Aztecs arrived, the local ruler sent an official to see how they were doing. The official found that the Aztecs were happy and content. He reported back to the ruler that the Aztecs had eaten all the rattlesnakes!

From about 1250 to 1300, the Aztecs were servants of the peoples who were already living by the Lake of the Moon. Things seemed to be going fine until the Aztecs offered a neighboring tribe's princess

---

[7] Many South American cities today are surrounded by squatters' shanty towns. People come in from the countryside. They cannot find work or a place to live, so they build small shacks on the outskirts of the city.

as a sacrifice. At that point, their neighbors forced them to move north, into the swamps of Lake Texcoco.

Mexico-Tenochtitlan

The Aztecs were still looking for a homeland. They didn't know where it was supposed to be. But they knew they would know it when they found it.

According to their legend, Huitzilopochtli had told them to look for a sign. When they saw an eagle, perched on a cactus and eating a snake, that was the place where they were to settle down.

When the Aztecs had to move north, they kept looking for the sign. Into the swamps they went. They came to two small islands, three miles from shore, in the middle of Lake Texcoco. And what did they see? They saw an eagle, perched on a cactus and eating a snake. This was their new homeland!

So, there in the swamps of Lake Texcoco, the Aztecs built their city. It was called *Mexico-Tenochtitlan* (meh-SHEE-co Ten-OTCH-tit-lan). Mexico means "The Town in the Middle of the Lake of the Moon." Tenochtitlan means "Place of the Prickly Pear Cactus." It was about the year 1325.

It might seem odd to build a city in the middle of a lake, but there are some advantages. Neither of the two islands had much soil. But the little soil that was there was very *fertile*—it was good for growing crops.

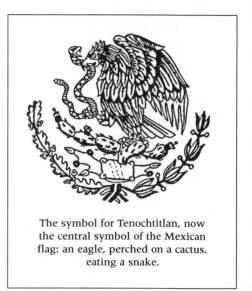

The symbol for Tenochtitlan, now the central symbol of the Mexican flag: an eagle, perched on a cactus, eating a snake.

And since the Aztecs were in the middle of the lake, it was easy for them to defend themselves against enemies.

Besides, the people in the cities nearby weren't interested in attacking the Aztecs. They figured the land the Aztecs were living on wasn't worth fighting for.

This land that wasn't worth fighting over is the place where Mexico City stands today. And the symbol on the Mexican flag is the symbol for Tenochtitlan—an eagle, standing on a cactus, eating a snake.

Question
• What is the symbol of Mexico? Why?

☀☺☀☺☀☺☀☺☀☺☀☺☀☺☀☺☀

1325-1440: The Empire Forms
At first, the Aztecs had only a few thousand people but their numbers grew quickly.

Other nations didn't pay much attention to the Aztecs at first. They didn't want to have anything to do with the Aztecs.

But these other nations fought against one another. And Tenochtitlan was smack in the middle between the nations that were fighting each other.

In 1426, the king of Tenochtitlan made an agreement with the leaders of three other cities: *Tlaltelolco* (tlahl-TELL-ol-co), *Tlacopan* (TLAH-co-pahn), and *Texcoco* (tesh-CAH-co). The leaders of the four cities decided to work together. Their armies joined together to fight against other cities in the area. Together, the Aztecs and their allies captured most of the other cities.

By 1428, the Aztecs and their allies had become the strongest powers in the region.

As a result Tenochtitlan, Tlacopan, and Texcoco formed what became known as the *Triple Alliance*.

At first, these cities merely agreed to defend one another. As it turned out, however, their agreement meant that Tenochtitlan became stronger and richer than the other cities.

Before the Alliance, Tenochtitlan was a weak city. The people there had been forced to pay tribute to other cities. They did not think they were very great. They were all equal and all equally not so great.

The enemies of the Aztecs thought they were worthless barbarians. They called the Aztecs "dog people."

But by the time the Triple Alliance was formed, Tenochtitlan and its allies had already conquered other cities. Tenochtitlan had become a powerful city and was able to demand tribute from other cities. And instead of all the people thinking of themselves as equals, the warriors were thought to be very important while farmers were considered unimportant.

And then the Aztecs began thinking they were great compared to the peoples they conquered. They thought Tenochtitlan was better than all the other cities.

When the Aztecs defeated another city, they destroyed the history books of that city. Why would they do that? They wanted to rewrite history to make themselves look better yet. This often happens when one people group conquers another. The conquerors want to talk only about their good points. They don't want history to record their bad points.

The Aztecs believed that their purpose was to conquer the nations around them, for the glory of Huitzilopochtli. Soon they conquered all the cities in the Valley of the Lake of the Moon.

Question
• What was the *Triple Alliance*?

1440-1521: Expansion

By the time the Aztecs had conquered everyone else in the Valley of the Lake of the Moon (also called the Valley of Mexico), they began to influence people throughout much of the area we now know as the country of Mexico.

During the Aztecs' entire history, there were only four major emperors.

Montezuma I ruled for twenty-eight years, from 1440 to 1468. He expanded the empire eastward to the coast of the Gulf of Mexico. As the empire expanded, the Aztecs in Tenochtitlan gained many wonderful products including chocolate, rubber, cotton, tropical fruits, and the feathers of rare birds. The conquered areas also provided victims (human beings) to sacrifice to Huitzilopochtli.

Under Montezuma I, Tenochtitlan became the Aztecs' military capital. It was the place where the army received its orders. Texcoco became the Aztecs' intellectual capital. It was the place where people went to get the best education.

The second Aztec emperor was *Axayacatl* (ah-SHY-ah-cahtl). He ruled only twelve years, from 1469 to 1481.

Axayacatl turned against Tlaltelolco, even though Tlaltelolco had been an ally of Tenochtitlan. He fought against the city and conquered it along with many other cities.

Ahuitzotl (ah-WEE-tsawtl) was the third emperor. He ruled for sixteen years, from 1486 to 1502.

His troops conquered the land to the west of Tenochtitlan. They conquered cities all the way to the Pacific Ocean and as far south as Mexico's present border with Guatemala.

Montezuma II was the last important Aztec emperor. He is also the most famous. He ruled from 1502 until 1521 or 1522. The army of Montezuma II took over even more area, so that the Aztec Empire grew even bigger. Montezuma II also broke the Triple Alliance.

Montezuma II

When the three cities first formed the Triple Alliance, they had made an agreement about who would receive the spoils of war. Spoils are the things that the army takes away from the enemy during a war. The leaders of the cities had agreed that the spoils of war would be divided into five parts.

Texcoco and Tenochtitlan would each get two parts, and Tlacopan would get one.

As time went on, the differences between Tlacopan and the other two cities became greater and greater. Texcoco and Tenochtitlan became richer and richer, as they received more goods after the wars.

Tlacopan was a weak city compared to Tenochtitlan. By the time Montezuma II became emperor, Tenochtitlan pretended that Tlacopan didn't even exist.

But Texcoco was weak, too. It had schools, and its citizens were well-educated. But their brains couldn't do much to save them when Tenochtitlan decided to attack. And that was just what happened. Tenochtitlan attacked. And when the battle was over, the people of Tenochtitlan had absolute power.

Questions
- Why did Tlacopan become weaker than Tenochtitlan?
- Why was Tenochtitlan able to defeat Texcoco?
- Locate Tenochtitlan on the map on page 76. Mexico City is now found at the same spot. Find Mexico City on a modern map.

🌞☺🌞☺ 🌞☺🌞☺🌞☺🌞☺ 🌞☺🌞☺🌞

Government

When the Aztecs conquered other cities, these cities became part of the Aztec Empire. But the people in these cities belonged to different tribes. Each city in the Aztec Empire belonged to a specific tribe. You would never find people from different tribes living together. Each tribe had its own spot.

At one point, the Aztecs ruled over twenty tribes. That was when the Aztec Empire was the greatest.

The different tribes had to pay tribute to the Aztecs, and they had to obey the Aztec rulers. The Aztecs placed tax gatherers in each of the tribes' leading cities. They also sent Aztec governors to these cities. If they believed a certain tribe might rebel against the Aztec leaders, they sent soldiers there "just in case."

The land where a particular tribe lived was owned by that tribe. Each tribe was allowed to rule itself—as long as they paid tribute to their Aztec rulers.

Each tribe had its own chiefs and its own councils. The council members were elected by the warriors. The council members distributed the land, made sure that children were properly educated, and made sure that the poor people had enough to eat. The council members also served as judges in court cases.

Judges in the Aztec Empire were very powerful. The Aztecs had no juries. And they didn't believe in prisons. If you did something wrong, nobody tried to help you to change. They figured you needed to be punished.

Once a judge heard a case, his decision was final.

Here are some typical punishments.[8] If you lied about your neighbors, your lips would be cut off. If you stole something, you would be tied to a post and all your neighbors would throw stones at you until you died. If you killed someone, you would either be strangled or have your head crushed by a large stone. If you became drunk and you were not a nobleman, you would either be beaten to death or strangled in public. If you became drunk and you were a nobleman, you would be drowned in private.

The kings of a tribe were called "chief speakers." The chief speaker was always elected by certain representatives of the tribe. During the early part of Aztec history, any man in the tribe could be elected as chief speaker. In later years, however, the chief speaker had to be a member of the royal family.

To the Aztecs, the tribe was more important than the individual or the family. It was important to be part of a particular tribe. But for many tribes, it was not so important to be part of the Aztec Empire.

The various cities had been forced to become part of the Aztec Empire because the Aztecs were more powerful than they were. They stayed in the empire because they were afraid of what would happen

---

[8] Lest the Aztecs seem worse than they were, perhaps we should point out that they never practiced torture the way the Europeans of their day did. Though the Aztecs' means of sacrifice were often grizzly, their victim's suffering was relatively brief, and was most certainly less painful than what was experienced by someone in Europe whose bones were pulled out of joint on the rack. . . .

if they rebelled against the Aztecs. It was fear rather than loyalty that kept the Aztec Empire together.

As a result, when the Spaniards eventually arrived in Aztec territory, they found that many cities were glad to break free of the Aztecs. When the opportunity came, the cities joined the Spaniards in fighting against the Aztecs.

War
Purpose

The Aztecs had a completely different idea about war than most people do today. We think of war as a disaster. It is bad. It's something we want to avoid. But the Aztecs were afraid of peace!

The Aztecs fought in the name of their god, Huitzilopochtli. They fought for his glory. They fought to extend the borders of his kingdom. And they fought to get him the food he needed. Without war, how could they get the captives they needed to sacrifice to him?

In the Old Testament we find that the people of Israel fought in the name of Yahweh. They fought for His glory, that His name might be known throughout the earth. This is why David fought Goliath (see I Samuel 17:45ff). Of course, Yahweh never needed "food." But He has commanded His people to do everything in His name and for His glory (Colossians 3:17).

When the Aztecs fought, they had three goals in mind.

First, they wanted prisoners. They would sacrifice the prisoners to feed their gods.

Second, the Aztecs wanted other people to pay tribute to them. They wanted something they could use to pay the priests and rulers in Tenochtitlan. The priests and rulers didn't grow crops, so they needed other people to provide food for them.

Third, the Aztecs wanted more people to worship Huitzilopochtli. The people who were conquered by the Aztecs were allowed to continue worshiping their old gods, but they had to worship Huitzilopochtli as well.

Most of the armies of the world today fight for different goals and for different gods. Their goals and gods are usually their governments and their own *form* of government.

The form of government in the United States is democracy. The U.S. Army fights for the glory and honor of the United States, for democracy, and for the United Nations. No one would dare suggest that the U.S. Army fights for Yahweh, for Jesus Christ, for Christianity, or for righteousness!

The armies of Muslim countries may be the only ones who actually fight *in the name of a god*. They fight "in the name of Allah."

As Christians, our purpose should always be to worship and glorify Yahweh. We should seek His kingdom and His righteousness in all the earth (Matthew 6:9-10, 33).

How They Fought

Before going to battle, the Aztecs were like the Incans. They would try to frighten their opponents into simply giving up.

First they would send a group of men from Tenochtitlan to visit the leaders of another city. The Aztecs would invite the other city to join their Mexican confederation.

"These are the only rules you must obey if you want to join us," they would say.

1. We will protect you.
2. You must worship Huitzilopochtli.
3. We must trade openly with one another.
4. You may keep your own chief, gods, customs, etc.
5. You must promise to obey the Mexican rulers.
6. You must refuse to deal directly with the rulers of any other area that is not part of the Mexican confederation.

"If you agree with these rules, you must prove it to us. You must give a large gift of gold, cotton or precious stones for the rulers of the three allied city-states." (Remember: Tenochtitlan and Texcoco got two portions each, and Tlacopan received one.)

These were the threats and rules that the Aztecs would give to the council members of the other city. The other city almost never responded immediately. They would wait for the men from Tenochtitlan to leave.

Before leaving, the Aztecs would give each member of the council at least one sword and one shield. If the Aztecs did eventually go to war with the other city, they wanted everyone to know that it would be a fair fight.

Twenty days later, after the men from Tenochtitlan visited the city, a group of men from Texcoco would visit. Texcoco was the second city in the Triple Alliance. The men from Texcoco brought even stronger threats.

"If you don't join us," they would say, "then your ruler will be killed and your warriors will be made into sacrifices. On the other hand, if you do join our confederation, you will only have to give us one small gift each year."

If the city council still refused to make a decision right away, then the Texcocans would put a headdress on the head of the city's chief. They would anoint the chief's head to give him strength in battle. And they would give all the members of the council more weapons.

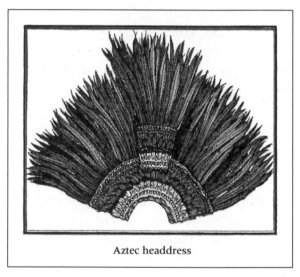

Aztec headdress

Twenty days later, if the city still had not given in, then a group of men from Tlacopan would go. Tlaco-pan was the third city in the Triple Alliance. The men from Tlacopan didn't go to the council. They spoke directly to the citizens of the city.[9]

The men from Tlacopan tried to make the people of the other city very confused and worried. Maybe if the people were scared enough, they would persuade their leaders to surrender to the Aztecs.

"If your city doesn't join our confederation," the men would say, "then you can expect a major disaster, destruction, death, and sacrifice. Instead of friendly relations, you will be forced to pay huge tributes. . . ."

When the men from Tlacopan had finished their speech, they would pass out more weapons. Then they left. Finally, after another twenty days, the Aztecs would declare war. Aztec wars were usually very short. One battle was almost all it ever took. When the Aztecs fought, they didn't try to kill their enemies. Instead, they tried to make sure their opponents were still alive when the battle was over. The Aztecs' goal was to take captives. The warriors gained glory by how many prisoners they took. Dead enemies didn't count.

What Happened After the Battle

As soon as the battle was over, a runner set off to Tenochtitlan to announce the news. Before the messenger even said anything, the people could tell whether or not it was a victory for the Aztecs.

If the Aztecs lost, the runner went with his hair hanging over his face.

If they won, he kept his hair bound up. To show everyone that there was a victory, he held his weapons high as he entered Tenochtitlan. The happy citizens of Tenochtitlan would welcome him with flowers, incense, and trumpets.

When the battle ended, the Aztecs counted how many of their own men had been killed. Then they sacrificed some of the captives. They put the other captives in cages to be sacrificed when they got back home to their own cities.

In the meantime, the leaders of the two armies discussed what each side would do for the other. The winners could demand whatever they wanted from the losers.

When the Aztecs won, they chose not to be too harsh, if the losers would promise to be faithful to the Aztec Empire.

During these discussions, the two sides would discuss how many slaves, how much wool, maize, gold or other valuables the losers would have to give each year.

Then the winners warned the losers: "See to it that you fulfill and keep the agreement. In some future time, do not say that this is

---

[9] This is similar to what the king of Assyria did in 2 Kings 18:17-36 and 2 Chronicles 32:9ff.

not what you agreed to. And do not say that you made these promises because someone lied to you. You know what kind of agreement you are making, and you must keep it."

In modern wars, if a man is captured, it is his duty to try to escape. Not so among the Aztecs and their enemies! As far as they were concerned, if a soldier was captured, he was supposed to go willingly to be sacrificed. To die as a prisoner was "more honorable than to return home as a fugitive." Any nobleman who had been captured and then escaped would be killed by his own people!

Questions

The Aztecs were like the Incans and the people of Yahweh in the Old Testament. They all fought wars for the glory of their gods and to extend the worship of their gods among other peoples.

- Do you think the Incans and the Aztecs *blessed* the peoples they conquered? Why or why not?
- How about the Hebrews in the Old Testament? Did they bless the nations they conquered? Why or why not? (See Deuteronomy 10:17-19; 24:17-22; Joshua 6:16-27; 8:18-35.)

Weapons and Armor

The Aztecs had a form of armor that was made of quilted cotton. It was about an inch thick. The cotton was soaked in salt water and then dried. The dried salt made the cotton extra hard.

The atl-atl, or spear-thrower, effectively extended the length of a man's arm, thus increasing the force and speed with which he could launch a spear

This armor was very effective against spears and arrows. In fact, it was so effective that the Spaniards began using it, too. They found that it protected them better than the metal armor they had brought with them. Cotton was also lighter and cooler than metal.

Besides their armor, most Aztec warriors carried round shields. The shields were 20 to 30 inches wide. They were made of wood and covered with leather or metal. Some soldiers had larger body shields.

The most common weapons were the javelin, the bow and arrow, the sling, and the two-edged sword. The tip of the javelin was made of either fire-hardened wood or a very hard, smooth rock called obsidian. The javelin was usually thrown using a special spear thrower called an atl-atl. Atl-atls could be as long as five feet almost as long as their users were tall! Some javelins had more than one point. Some were like harpoons, with a cord for pulling it back after it had been thrown.

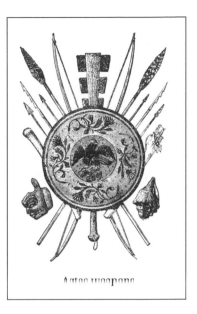

Aztec weapons

Aztec bows were sometimes as long as five feet. The arrows had tips made of either bone, obsidian, or fire-hardened wood.

The Aztecs' slings could throw stones the size of eggs.

The two-edged swords had three-foot long hardwood blades with obsidian edges. They were so sharp and strong that they could cut off the head of a horse with one stroke. In fact, they were so sharp, the warriors could shave with them. The only problem with these swords was that the blades lost their edges rather easily and the obsidian then needed to be replaced.

Questions
- What is an *atl-atl*.
- What is a *javelin*?
- What were the weaknesses of Aztec weapons?

- What are some of the differences between warfare among the Aztecs and modern warfare?

❉☺❉☺❉☺❉☺❉☺❉☺❉☺❉☺❉

Effectiveness of the Aztec Army

Even though the Aztecs had allies who "protected" them, they had no friends. And although the Aztecs were powerful, they could not conquer everyone.

For example, the Tarascans lived to the west of the Aztecs. They defeated the Aztec king Axayacatl who reigned from 1469-1481. After that defeat, the Aztecs never attacked the Tarascans again.

The *Tlaxcalans* (tlash-CAH-lans) were the ones who had helped the Aztecs gain independence. But they were eventually surrounded by the Aztecs. There was constant war between the Aztecs and the Tlaxcalans, but the Aztecs never conquered the Tlaxcalans.

To help defend themselves against the Aztecs, the Tlaxcalans built a stone wall around their entire territory! It was twenty feet wide and nine feet high.

Commerce

Aztec cities, towns, and villages tended to be large compared to those of the Incan Empire, so trade was much more common among the Aztecs than among the Incans. Tenochtitlan had possibly the largest open-air market in the world. As many as 60,000 people traded there each day!

Even though there was a lot of trading going on, the Aztec economy was based on agriculture and barter, just like the Incan economy. The Aztecs did not have money like we have. But a few items— feather capes, quills filled with gold dust, and cacao beans[10]—were always considered valuable.

---

[10] Cacao beans grow on a tree. Cocoa comes from cacao beans.

Personal Life
Growing Up

For the first few years of life, Aztec boys and girls just watched what their parents did. At about age four, they were expected to join in the work. They didn't have to do very hard work at that age, but they were expected to learn how to help their families. Boys might carry water from the well. Girls had to learn the names of everything in a woman's work basket.

The way a person cut his hair told a lot about him. Little boys had their heads shaved. When he had his tenth birthday, he was allowed to grow a tuft of hair in back.

A boy could not become a citizen of the empire until he became a man. And he could not become a man until he had captured at least one enemy warrior for sacrifice. If he killed an enemy warrior, it meant nothing. An enemy had to be taken alive in order to provide blood for the gods. And, of course, providing blood for the gods was the whole purpose of life for the Aztecs.

Once a young man had captured his first enemy, he was allowed to change his hairstyle. Then he could wear a lock of hair over his right ear. After he had captured four prisoners, he was allowed to grow a pigtail.

If a boy did not capture an enemy in his first three battles, other people would make fun of him. Everywhere he went he would hear people saying, "What a coward! What a woman! You haven't caught a prisoner yet? Why, you're just a little boy!"

A young man did *not* want to hear people mock him like this. So he would do anything he could to capture a prisoner of war.

Questions
- What did an Aztec boy have to do in order to become a man?
- Why do you think, from the Aztecs' perspective, it was important that a boy should do this thing?
- Can you think of any similar thing(s) a boy must do in your country in order to be thought of as a mature man, ready for marriage?

- From your perspective, why is it important that a boy in your country should do the thing(s) he must do in order to be thought of as a mature man, ready for marriage?
- From a biblical perspective, do you think there is anything else a boy should do before he should be thought of as a mature man, ready for marriage?

☼☺☼☺☼☺☼☺☼☺☼☺☼☺☼☺☼

Men's and Women's Roles

There was one other thing that a young man had to do in order to really be an adult. He had to get married. Before he was married, a young man had no land of his own. Once a couple was married, they were given a plot of land to cultivate.

Aztec men worked as farmers or craftsmen. They also built the houses. The women made the meals, cared for the children, wove cloth, made clothes, tended the kitchen garden, and looked after the livestock.

An Aztec proverb said that men preferred wives with "both ears plugged and their mouths sewn shut." You can see that husbands and wives did not expect to be great friends!

Before an Aztec girl was married, she was not allowed to talk to boys. In fact, she couldn't even look at a boy. If she was caught talking to a boy or look- ing at a boy, she would be severely punished. Her parents had to throw chili peppers in a fire and hold her head in the smoke so her eyes and lungs would burn from the fumes.

Farmer using a digging stick

(This wouldn't kill her, of course. But it

would cause so much pain that she would never do such a thing again.)

Questions

- Do you think Aztec men had a good view about women? Why or why not?
- Do you think it was a good idea to hold girls over a fire filled with chili peppers? Why or why not?
- Do you see any problems with men's or women's attitudes toward one another in your culture? Why or why not?

🌟☺🌟☺🌟☺🌟☺🌟☺🌟☺🌟☺🌟☺🌟

Marriage

A man was expected to get married at about age 20. Women married at about age 16.

When it was time for an Aztec man to marry, his father would look for a wife for him. The father would talk to neighboring clans to see if they had any young women who were ready to marry.

Once the father had found a young woman who seemed like she would make a good wife for his son, he would talk to a matchmaker. The matchmaker was an old woman. The father would ask the old woman to talk to the young woman's parents.

So the old woman would visit the young woman's parents, and ask them to let their daughter marry the man's son.

"Oh, no!" the girl's parents would protest. "No! This will never do! Why, look at her! She is still just a girl. She would never do as so-and-so's wife! She barely knows how to cook. . . ." But their answers were all just part of being polite.

Then the matchmaker would go back to the young man's parents and tell them what the young woman's parents had said.

A few days later, the young man's father would send the match-maker back to the girls' family again. This time, he sent along many presents for the matchmaker to give to the young woman's parents.

At that point, the young woman's parents would agree. They would receive the gifts. And they would tell the matchmaker what they would give to the young man for marrying their daughter.

Now the young man's parents called a priest, and told him the birthdates of the young man and the young woman. It was the priest's job to figure out a "lucky" day for the wedding.

Aztec weddings began with a large feast at the bride's home. Guests brought gifts for the new couple. During the wedding feast, elders in the community gave speeches. They told the groom and the bride what their responsibilities would be as husband and wife: what they would have to do for each other and what they had to do for the larger society.

When evening came, everybody went to the groom's home. The matchmaker had to carry the bride on her back. (The Aztecs thought it was bad luck for the bride to touch the ground between her parents' home and the home of her husband-to-be.)

Man carving and woman weaving

When the couple arrived at the groom's home, they were set beside each other on two sleeping mats. More people gave speeches. Then the matchmaker tied a corner of the groom's cloak to the tail of the bride's blouse. At this point, they were husband and wife.

Before an Aztec couple had children, their marriage was not complete. If a couple could not have any children, everyone thought it was a tragedy. This usually led to divorce.

Questions
- Describe an Aztec wedding.
- Compare an Aztec wedding to a wedding in your culture.
- Can you think of any especially good customs in the Aztec wedding? Explain why you think they were good.
- Are there any parts of an Aztec wedding that you think might be wrong or bad? Explain why you think they were bad.

• What about good or bad practices in weddings in your own culture?

Mexico-Tenochtitlan

The City of Tenochtitlan

Several things impressed the Spaniards when they came to Tenochtitlan. One was the city's size. There were between 200,000 and 350,000 people living in Tenochtitlan. The city included close to 60,000 homes.

It was far bigger than any city in Europe at the time. London, Rome, and Venice were the largest cities in Europe back then. They had populations of close to 100,000 people each. Seville, a city in Spain, was the largest city the Spaniards would have known. It had maybe 60,000 people. So Tenochtitlan was much bigger than any of the cities that the Spaniards had ever seen.

Not only was Tenochtitlan large, it was a marvel of engineering. The Aztecs had built three big roads across the swampy lake that connected their island home to the shore. This type of road, raised up above the water, is called a *causeway*. Each causeway was two or three miles long and wide enough for ten horsemen to ride across side by side.

The Aztecs also made two pipes to carry fresh water to the center of the city. And they built a ten-mile long dike to protect the city from flooding.

Much of the land on which the city was built used to be part of the lake. But the Aztecs had found ways to *reclaim* land from the lake. That is, they found ways to take parts of the lake and make solid land out of it.

They did this in two ways. First, over the years, the Aztecs wove hundreds of huge reed baskets, eight feet wide by fifty feet long. They would connect these baskets end-to-end in long strips. Then they would anchor them to the bottom of the lake.

After they had anchored the baskets to the bottom, the Aztecs would then fill them with mud. They would plant willow trees along the edges of the mud-filled baskets, and maize and other crops in the rest of the mud.

Eventually, the roots of the willow trees would grow through the bottoms of the reed boats in which they had been planted. When the roots went into the bottom of the lake, the willow trees became permanent anchors. That is, the roots of the willow trees held the baskets firmly to the bottom of the lake.

The farmers kept planting crops in the mud-filled baskets. With each crop, the farmers would add more dirt on top of the garden that was already there. This would slowly sink the garden until it had become a rectangular strip of solid land.

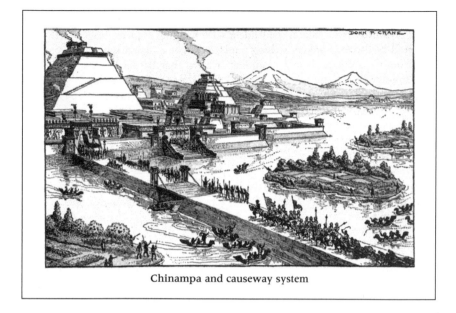

Chinampa and causeway system

The Aztecs had a second method of reclaiming land from the lake. They would set posts in two parallel rows in the bottom of the lake. Then they would dig a ditch on the outside of the two rows of posts. They would pile the dirt from these ditches in the strip between the posts. The posts held the dirt in place.

Once the dirt was high enough, the Aztecs would plant willows along the edge. As with the reed boats, the willows would then help anchor the gardens and prevent the soil from being washed back into the lake.

The strips of reclaimed land were called *chinampas*.

Questions
• Describe a *chinampa*.
• Explain how the Aztecs made their two small islands grow bigger over the years until they could support a large city.

Hygiene

Besides the size of the city and its technological marvels, there was one more thing that impressed the Spaniards. That was the Aztecs' cleanliness. The Spaniards noticed how clean the people were, and they noticed how clean the whole city looked.

Although the temple in the center of Tenochtitlan was filthy, and the priests' hair was usually caked with blood, the rest of the city was clean. And normal citizens took baths at least once a day. (Montezuma washed twice daily.)

It wasn't like that in Europe. Europeans at the time were filthy. People in Europe almost never bathed. One of the queens of Sweden is known to have been proud of the fact that her hands were black because she never washed them!

The Aztecs didn't use soap to bathe. If they were in the lake, they used the roots of certain plants that produced a lather. Soaptree was one plant like that. Something like soap can be found in the roots and trunk of a soaptree.

The Aztecs also used sweatlodges for cleaning themselves. Every Aztec home had a sweatlodge. It was a small igloo-shaped hut built into one of the walls. The Aztecs would light a fire that heated one wall of the sweatlodge until it was red hot. Then they would creep inside, throw water on the wall to produce steam, and allow themselves to be sweat-and-steam cleaned.

In the city of Tenochtitlan, there were more than a thousand sweeper/washers hard at work every day keeping the houses and streets clean.

Garbage was buried at the edge of the city. This was different from what the people of London did at the time. In London, garbage was tossed into the streets and left there to rot.

Tenochtitlan even had public toilets near the roads. They were spaced evenly along all the roadways. The sewage that came from these toilets was used as fertilizer.

Questions
• Describe an Aztec sweatlodge.

• The Spaniards were very positively impressed with many things about Aztec culture. List three or four achievements that impressed the Spaniards. Then explain why they were so amazing.

🌟☺🌟☺🌟☺🌟☺🌟☺🌟☺🌟☺🌟☺🌟

Housing

The cottages that Aztec farmers lived in were simple buildings. They were built of wood, straw and mud. They had one room, a dirt floor, an open doorway, no windows and no chimney.

Craftsmen and merchants lived in fancier houses. Their houses were built of bricks. The bricks were made of clay, and baked in the sun. This type of brick is called *adobe* (uh-DOE-bee). The adobe houses were one story tall and had four or five rooms built around a garden-courtyard.

Government officials and the very wealthiest merchants lived in stone houses that were painted with a clay paint. Some were painted white. Others were painted red.

The Chief Speaker's palace was best of all. It had 100 rooms, 100 steam baths, 20 entrances, and a main hall that held 3,000 people. Its walls were covered in marble, jasper, and other rare materials. Its ceilings were made of carved pine and cedar. It had irrigated gardens and specially planted trees and flowers. It even had zoos filled with exotic animals, and aviaries filled with birds.

Aztec pottery

The Aztecs' belongings were very simple. The women used straw brooms, baskets, and clay jars. The men used wooden digging sticks instead of plows. Most Aztecs had no chairs or beds. They used straw mats for sitting and sleeping.

Some very wealthy people owned a wooden chair or two, but even the Chief Speaker slept on a straw mat.

Clothing

All of the Aztec men wore a loin cloth (a piece of fabric that covered their private areas; see the picture of the spear thrower on page 88). If they could afford a cloak, they might also wear that. An Aztec cloak was a piece of fabric in the shape of a rectangle. To put it on, you would place it under your left armpit and then tie it in a knot over your right shoulder (see page 81). Richer men wore many cloaks. And the priests and warriors wore tunics.

Common people wore clothing made of white cloth. The upper classes were allowed to wear colors and designs. Each class, however, had its own specific colors. Turquoise, for

Traditional ceremonial garb

instance, was the color of royalty. Only the Chief Speaker was allowed to put on a turquoise cloak. Anyone found wearing the wrong color could be put to death.

Common people went barefoot. Those who were richer were permitted to wear sandals.

Questions
- How were Aztec clothes different from the clothes you wear?
- How did the Aztecs use clothing to help distinguish people from one another?

- Do people in your culture use clothing to distinguish themselves from other people? If so, how, when, and where?
- Did people in the "olden days" use clothing to distinguish themselves from one another?

☀☺☀☺☀☺☀☺☀☺☀☺☀☺☀☺☀

Jewelry and Cosmetics

Little boys had their earlobes punctured. And not only that—they had their lower lips and their noses punctured, too. Their noses were punctured in the center portion, and also in the wings of their nostrils. They would stretch all these holes until ornaments could be stuck in them.

Warriors put different kinds of feathers and stones in these holes to show what kind of job they had in the army. You could tell if a man was a great army leader by looking at his ears, nose, and lips.

Besides clothing, hairstyles, and jewelry, the Aztecs had many different cosmetics. Yellow was their favorite color. Aztec women would put a yellowish ointment on their faces, to make them look more yellow. This yellow ointment was called *axin*. To make axin, they would cook and crush a certain type of insect. Axin was kind of waxy, and was also used as a salve against chapped lips. It really worked, too!

The Aztecs used perfumes, incense, and rose water. And they had a chewing gum to sweeten their breath.

They even had mirrors made of iron pyrite and obsidian!

Questions

- Some people think ear plugs and nose rings are ugly and perhaps sinful or demonic. What do you think and why?
- Do you have the same opinion about pierced earrings? Why or why not?

- Does the Bible have anything to say about such practices? (Look up Leviticus 19:28 and Deuteronomy 14:1ff; also Acts 10:9-16 and Romans 14:20.)

☀☺☀☺☀☺☀☺☀☺☀☺☀☺☀☺☀

Food

The Aztecs ate a lot of maize. (Remember that maize is a type of corn.) To prepare maize for eating, Aztec women would let it sit in lime water overnight. Then they would boil it and grind it into flour. They used a small stone table called a *metate* (meh-TAH-tay) for grinding the maize.

The Aztecs used maize to make *tortillas* (tore-TEE-uhs). The tortillas were in the shape of a circle, about twelve inches across, and very thin. The women baked them on a griddle.

Tortillas were the main food of the Aztecs. The women made them fresh for each meal. A three-year-old child ate about half a tortilla each day. A five-year-old ate about one whole tortilla each day. A thirteen-year-old ate two.

They also used maize to make *atole* (ah-TOLE-ay)—a kind of porridge. Sometimes the Aztecs would pour *maguey* (MAW-gway) syrup on their corn porridge, or they would sweeten it with honey.

Another way the women used maize was to make *tamales* (tuh-MAHL-ays). Tamales are steamed maize stuffed with something else. That something else could be fruit, beans, mushrooms, fish, rabbit, turkey eggs, frogs, snails, beeswax, tadpoles, or baby salamanders. But whatever they decided to stuff in a tamale, it had a lot of seasoning!

Besides growing maize, the Aztecs also farmed tomatoes, avocados, beans, and a type of grain called *amaranth*.

They ate water creatures, too. They ate fish, shrimp, and the eggs of water flies and other water insects. The Aztecs thought these insect eggs were a treat. They enjoyed them as much as you might enjoy eating chocolate M&M's or a dish of ice cream!

Sometimes the Aztecs also ate birds, turkeys, and dogs.

The poor people had water to drink. The rich people, however, drank chocolate. In fact, Europeans had never heard of chocolate until they came to America and bumped into the Aztecs! To make chocolate, the Aztecs pounded *cacao* (cuh-COW) beans. (Notice that they are not called cocoa beans, but *cacao* beans. Cocoa powder and chocolate come from cacao beans.) The Aztecs boiled the beans in water with a little bit of maize flour, and whipped it all up until it was thick and frothy. They flavored the chocolate with honey, vanilla, and other spices. By the time it was ready to drink, the chocolate melted in their mouths.

There was one drink that not many Aztecs wanted to drink. It was called *octli*. Octli was alcohol made from maguey sap. The reason most Aztecs wouldn't drink it was because they didn't want to get drunk. Drunkenness was not allowed in Aztec society. If you became drunk, you would be put to death.

Questions
- What is *maize*?
- What is a *metate*?
- Describe a *tortilla*.
- Describe a *tamale*.
- Maize was the staple, or the main food ingredient, for the Aztecs. What is the staple in the United States? *(wheat)* What is the staple in Japan and China? *(rice)*

☀☺☀☺☀☺☀☺☀☺☀☺☀☺☀☺☀

Amusements

It appears that the Aztecs made more group music than the Incans. They also danced, did drama, and played more sports than the Incans did.

Performing Arts
The records show that Montezuma had singers, dancers, clowns, dwarfs, hunchbacks, jugglers, stilt dancers, and acrobats in his court.

Music

When you listen to a band, you hear different *types* of instruments. You hear *melodic* instruments, like a trumpet or a flute. When these instruments are played, you hear different notes. You can hear a melody—something you can sing.

Usually a band also has *percussive* instruments, like a drum or a cymbal. These instruments are used to keep the beat. They don't have a melody, but they might make you want to tap your feet or clap your hands.

Most of the Aztecs' instruments were percussive. They had drums, gongs, rattles, and bells. Dancers attached copper bells to their clothing and wore strings of jangling shells, bones, or dried nuts to add to the sounds.

They did have a few melodic instruments, though. They had trumpets made out of conch shells. They had clay whistles. And they had flutes. The flutes were six to eight inches long. They were made of clay or, sometimes, bamboo or bone. Most Aztec flutes could only play five notes, but a few types could play as many as sixteen notes.

Then, of course, there were the singers' voices.

The Aztecs didn't just make music for fun. They were very serious about it!

Aztec dancers and musicians as portrayed in the *Codex Florentino*. Instruments include an upright drum, a two-tone wooden gong, and several rattles.

Bernardino de Sahagun, a Spaniard who wrote about how the Aztecs lived, said: "If the singers did something amiss . . . ; or he who intoned the song spoiled it; or the leader marred the dance—

then the ruler commanded that they place in jail whoever had done the wrong; they imprisoned him, and he died."

Why did the Aztecs have such harsh punishment for those who made a mistake in a song? It was because music and dancing were very important in the Aztec religion. In fact, the Spaniards were so concerned about the connection between the Aztecs' religion and their songs and dances that in 1555 they made the following rule:

"The Indians shall not sing the . . . chants of their rites or ancient histories, without first having the said chants examined by the Clergy, or by people that understand the language very well. The ministers of the Gospel shall see that there is nothing profane in such chants."

Sports and Games

The Aztecs liked one particular sport much more than all others. They called this sport *tlachtli* (TLAHCH-tlee), meaning hipball. It was somewhat like soccer and basketball mixed together.

The playing field was shaped like a capital "I." The main court was like the long part of the "I." This part was 200 feet long and 30 feet wide. The endzones were like the top and bottom crossbeams of the "I." The court was surrounded by 15-foot high walls.

In the modern game of basketball, we have hoops on both ends of the court. The hoops are ten feet above the floor. In tlachtli, two stone rings were set in the walls halfway between the two end zones. There was one ring on each side of the court. The rings were about ten feet above the ground.

A big difference between tlachtli and basketball was the direction that the ball would go through the hoop or ring. In basketball, the ball goes through the hoop vertically—from up to down. It is thrown up above the hoop, and goes down through the hoop.

In tlachtli, the ball went through the ring horizontally—from one side to the other. The rings were set so you could look through them like windows. The ball could come toward the ring from either end of the court, and go through the ring as it traveled down the court.

But, actually, this didn't happen very often. It was very hard to put the ball through a ring. The tlachtli ball was six inches in diameter, and made of solid rubber. It was quite heavy. The rings were just a little more than six inches across. So the ball would have to come at the ring just right in order to squeeze through it.

If you think shooting a basketball through a basketball hoop is difficult, you can imagine that it was almost impossible for a tlachtli player to get the ball to go through one of the rings!

Besides that, the tlachtli players weren't allowed to throw the ball!

So how did they play the game?

The object of tlachtli was to drive the ball into the other team's end zone. In order to do this, the players could hit the ball with their hips, elbows, knees, and buttocks.

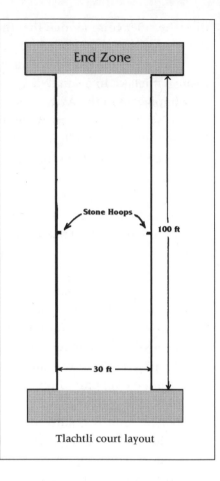

Tlachtli court layout

They wore special clothes to protect themselves. They had leather belts stuffed with cotton, and pads for their hands and knees. But even though they tried to protect themselves, players were often hurt very badly. In fact, tlachtli players would often die either from getting hit by the ball (because the ball was so heavy), or from exhaustion.

If anybody drove the ball through one of the rings, their team won the game immediately. That was the end of the game.

When a game ended like that, the spectators tried to get away as fast as they could. Why? Because the player who drove the ball through the hoop was given a special reward: he could take all the clothes and possessions of the spectators. It was a literal example of "winner takes all"!

Of course, it was hard for the winner to get much of anything since everybody scrambled for the exit as soon as the game ended. But the player and his friends still tried to grab as many people as they could.

One time, there was a big tlachtli tournament between Tenochtitlan and Texcoco. This is what happened.

Nezahualpilli (NEH-tzah-wall-PEEL-ee) was the ruler of Texcoco at that time, and Montezuma was the ruler of Tenochtitlan. Nezahualpilli told Montezuma that his astrologers were predicting strangers would soon come to rule over Mexico. Montezuma said there was no way someone could overthrow his kingdom.

Nezahualpilli then bet Montezuma that his astrologers were right. "Let my men play your men in a best-of-five tlachtli tournament," said Nezahualpilli. "I will give you my kingdom if our team loses. If your team loses, you must give me three turkeys."

Montezuma took him up on the bet.

The first two games went to Montezuma's team. It looked certain that Nezahualpilli would

Sun calendar possibly used by the astrologers and also by the priests.

lose. But the team from Texcoco won the next three games in a row. That was three out of five. The Texcoco team had won the tournament.

Montezuma only had to give Nezahualpilli three turkeys. Yet he left the tlachtli court a very worried man. He was not worried about losing a tournament. He was worried about losing his kingdom. Nezahualpilli had won the bet that his astrologers' prediction was true. That meant strangers would soon come and overthrow Montezuma's kingdom.

And, as it turned out, that is what happened.

There was one other game that the Aztecs liked maybe even as much as tlachtli. It was called *patolli* (puh-TOLE-ee). Patolli was a board game similar to backgammon. The Aztecs used it for gambling. Playing patolli ruined the lives of many people. They lost houses, slaves, jewels, clothing, everything.

Question
• Describe *tlachtli*.

☀☺☀☺☀☺☀☺☀☺☀☺☀☺☀☺☀

Slavery[e]

The Aztecs' laws on slavery were much kinder than those practiced here in the United States.

In the United States, slaves were considered to be property. Just like land and houses, slaves could be inherited. When a slave owner died, his children would inherit the slaves.

Not only were the slaves themselves property, but the slaves' wives and children were their masters' property as well. If you were a slave in the United States, your master had the right to sell your children, your husband, or your wife. And you had no right to complain to anyone if he did so.

The United States had no legal limit on the number of years a slave would have to serve his master. There wasn't even any limit on how long his children and grandchildren would be slaves. They were born slaves and they would die slaves.

There was no law concerning how a slave could gain freedom, either. If the master happened to be especially kindhearted, a slave might gain his freedom. But most masters were not this kindhearted. So, without any laws to help them, most slaves would never go free.

In Aztec society, slaves could only be slaves for a short period of time. The master and the slave would agree upon a certain length of

Note For Adults:[e]

Many people have argued that certain forms of slavery are legitimate—specifically indentured servitude (the kind of arrangement by which many poor Europeans purchased passage to America) and temporary slavery to pay for debt and/or as a means by which a criminal may restore to his or her victims what s/he has taken.

Chattel slavery as practiced in the United States prior to the Civil War, however, is wholly illegitimate. (See Gary North, *Tools of Dominion: The Case Laws of Exodus* (Tyler, TX: The Institute for Christian Economics, 1990), pp. 232ff; also "A Biblical Argument Against American Slavery" by William Edgar and "R.L. Dabney's Defense of Virginia Revisited" by Steve Wilkins, both in *Chalcedon Report*, No. 369, April 1996.)

North argues his case on the basis that 1) Jesus annulled the Old Testament jubilee provisions, among which were the laws permitting "permanent" chattel slavery of foreigners (Luke 4:16-21; Leviticus 25:44-46); 2) "the slave family [in America] had no legal existence, yet . . . the family as created by God is . . . a covenant institution, and the heart of the covenant is legal" (North, p. 234); 3) "the Bible's hierarchical appeals court system was denied to slaves, for the legal hierarchy, upward and downward, ended with the slave-owner" (North, p. 239); 4) "there was no [legally recognized] way . . . for a slave to buy his way out of slavery" (North, p. 240).

Whether a slave "husband" and "wife" were permitted to live together and raise their children, or whether they might be separated forever was a matter decided wholly at the will and pleasure of their master(s). (Notice that I placed the words husband and wife in quotes—because Southern law permitted no such categories among slaves.) A slave "husband" had no recourse against his master if the master decided to engage in sexual activities with the slave's "wife."

William Edgar points out that the Reformed Presbyterian Church in the United States of America, from 1800 on, would not permit church members to hold slaves. Some of the argu

(cont. on next pg.)

ments for this position: 1) Virtually all African slaves had been made slaves through kidnapping or, as the King James Version puts it, "man-stealing." Exodus 21:16 says, "Anyone who kidnaps another and either sells him or still has him when he is caught must be put to death." Even if the owner of stolen goods doesn't actually do the stealing, he is guilty along with the thief if he knows that the goods are stolen. 2) Leviticus 24:22 tells us that the alien is to be under the same law as the native citizen. "At a minimum, that meant that if they embraced the God of Israel, they would have the same right to freedom as the Israelite after six years" (Edgar, pg. 10).

time. When that time period was over, the slave was free. The families of slaves were always free. And slaves themselves could buy their freedom.

There was another way that a slave could gain his freedom in Aztec society. If a slave was brought to the marketplace to be sold, he could gain his freedom if he was able to run fast enough! It was almost like a game of tag. And everyone had to play by the rules. Here's how it worked.

The slave had to run from the slave market into the Chief Speaker's palace without being caught by his owner or his owner's son(s). If he could get from the slave market to the palace without being caught, he would be set free immediately. Only the owner and his family were allowed to try to catch the slave. The other people in the marketplace could not stop the slave, and they could not stop the owner or his son(s) either.

There were two types of slavery in Aztec society. In one type of slavery, a person was forced to be a slave against his will.

Only certain groups of people were ever forced to be slaves. Aztecs who were convicted thieves or debtors often became slaves whether they liked it or not. People who were given to the Aztecs as tribute by one of the conquered cities had no choice about it either. If they were given as slaves, slaves they would be. Prisoners of war who had special skills might also be made slaves. (Other prisoners without any special skills were sacrificed to Huitzilopochtli.) In the other type of slavery, a person sold him- or herself into slavery. If there was a bad famine, for example, a person could say, "I will work for you for a year, if you will give me food, clothing and shelter." In this type of slavery, parents could also sell their children. Some parents did this because they needed food, or seeds to plant.

This second type of slavery is similar to what was practiced in Europe from the mid-1600s to the mid-1800s. It is also called indentured servitude. Many Europeans allowed themselves to be indentured servants so that they could come to America.

As far as the Aztecs were concerned, it was no shame to be a slave. Aztec women often married slaves. Itzcoatl, one of the Aztec's greatest rulers, was the son of a slave woman.

If a master hurt or killed his slave, he himself had to be killed.

If an Aztec slave was lazy or disobedient, he or she could be sold. If this happened three times, there were no more chances. The next step was to be put in a cage and sold for sacrifice.

Questions

• According to the Bible, why was slavery as practiced in the United States wrong?
• How did the Aztecs treat slaves better than they were treated in the United States?

☀☺☀☺☀☺☀☺☀☺☀☺☀☺☀☺☀

History—Part 2

By A.D. 1517, the Aztecs had conquered an area of 80,000 square miles. Their empire stretched from the Atlantic Ocean on the east to the Pacific Ocean on the west. And it went from *Oaxaca* (wah-HAH-cah) in the south to the desert in the north.

The Aztecs received tribute from over 15 million people. But these people did not like being ruled by the Aztecs. They itched for the day when the Aztecs would be defeated.

From the Aztecs' perspective, things couldn't have been better. It had been several years since Nezahualpilli had made his bet with Montezuma that strangers would come to take over Mexico. Since then, Nezahualpilli had died. Montezuma was now the ruler not only of Tenochtitlan, but also of Nezahualpilli's city—Texcoco.

Montezuma was in a stronger position than he had ever been before. In fact, he was the strongest Aztec ruler in history. He commanded an army of over 200,000 soldiers. If Montezuma needed these soldiers to go to war, they could be ready within 24 hours of getting their orders.

But then the omens came, omen upon omen. There were so many omens, in fact, that Montezuma didn't know which came first. And all the omens were bad.

People who believe in omens believe they foretell something about the future. They believe a "good omen" means something good will happen, and a "bad omen" means something bad will happen.

There were comets in the skies. And there was a fire in Huitzilopochtli's temple. No one knew what had caused it, and no one had been able to put it out. And there were many deformed babies. More babies were born with defects than anyone could remember. Then there was that windless day when the water rose in the lake and flooded the city. Why? No one knew.

Finally, there was the voice that people had heard at night. It sounded like the voice of a woman. They had heard her crying: "O my beloved sons, now we are at the point of going. My beloved sons, where shall I take you?"

The sense of dread and doom hung heavily over the city of Tenochtitlan.

The people were greatly afraid. What would happen to them?

. . . We'll find out later, after we have studied the Mayans.

Mayan Territory in Central America

Mayans

We know less about the Mayans than we do about either the Incans or the Aztecs. One of the reasons is that the Mayans' civilization had almost disappeared by the time the Spaniards arrived.

But people who study the ruins of ancient civilizations have dug around and found things that the Mayans used. They have found Mayan pottery, jewelry, statues, and other objects. People who dig in old ruins to see what they can find are called archaeologists.

Some of the things that have been found tell us about Mayan history. For example, archaeologists have found stones with inscriptions and other markings on them. The stones are set upright, and are used to remember someone or something. These types of stones are called *stelae* (STEEL-ay).[1]

A stela found by archaeologists in the 1930s.

Most of what we know about the Mayans comes from what the archaeologists have found.

---

[1] A gravestone is an example of a stela. Can you think of other stelae you have either seen or heard about? (Hint: How about the Washington Monument?)

History

The Mayans came before either the Incans or the Aztecs. Archaeologists have found Mayan settlements that were in existence more than a thousand years before Jesus came to earth. That's more than 3,000 years ago.

These early Mayan settlements were rather simple. This was the time when the Mayans were becoming great. It was the Mayans' "Formative Period." We don't know exactly when this period began (except that it was more than 3,000 years ago). But it lasted up until about A.D. 300.

After the Formative Period came the "Classic Period." That was when the Mayans *were* great. It lasted from about A.D. 300 to 925. During this time, the Mayans built large and beautiful cities and temples.

Sometime around A.D. 925, the Mayans' civilization stopped being so great. No one knows exactly what happened. What we do know is that they stopped building cities. They even abandoned a few of their cities for almost fifty years. This period is the "Inter-

Comb of Dovecote: An example of the size and intricacy of classical Mayan architecture. You can see one of the pyramids in the distance.

Regnum." It means the period "between reigns" or "between powers." It lasted from about A.D. 925 to 975.

Then, from A.D. 975 until the mid-1400s, the Mayans began building towns and cities again. (In a few places, they kept building until the early 1500s.) It was a time when the Mayan culture was growing again—especially in the Yucatan area of Mexico. This was the Mayans' "Post-Classic Period." The Mayans were strong, but not as strong as they had been back in the Classic Period.

After the Spaniards came, there were no more "classic" or "post-classic" periods. Like the Incans and the Aztecs, the Mayans no longer had a great civilization.

Questions
- What was the *Formative Period?*
- What was the *Classic Period?*
- What was the *Inter-Regnum?*
- What was the *Post-Classic Period?*

Religion

When it came to religion, the Mayans were just like the Incans and the Aztecs. Religion affected every area of their lives. It controlled their government. It played a part in what they bought, what they sold, their fairs, their feasts, their dances, their ball games, . . . everything.

Religious Workers

The Mayan priests offered sacrifices. They were also teachers. They were the ones who knew the Mayan counting system. And they knew the Mayan *glyphs.*

What are glyphs? Well, the Mayans, like so many other peoples, did not use an alphabet. In English, the letters of the alphabet stand for certain *sounds.* Glyphs are not letters, and they do not stand for sounds. Glyphs are symbols that stand for certain *meanings.*

For example, if you write "t-r-e-e," you are using an alphabet. If you draw a symbol that looks like a tree, you are using a glyph. Even if you draw a symbol that doesn't *look* like a tree, but *means* tree, you are using a glyph.

Some Mayan priests interpreted omens. For instance, if a couple was planning to get married, a priest would tell them what day would be best for the wedding. The priests would tell people what caused their sicknesses, decide what sacrifices were supposed to be offered, and determine if someone had been cursed through witchcraft.

So Mayan priests knew the glyphs. In other words, they knew how to read and write. And they taught these skills.

From what archaeologists can tell, the Mayan priests and

Chief priest with headdress

priestesses inherited their responsibilities. They were not elected or chosen for these jobs. The men and women who served in the priestly orders served because they were born into priestly families.[a]

Question
• What are *glyphs*?

Note For Adults:[a]

These priests were similar to the "magicians and wise men" who were in Pharaoh's court (see Genesis 41:8). They were also similar to the "magicians, enchanters, astrologers and diviners" in the courts of the Babylonian kings (see Daniel 5:11).

Of course, as Christians, we know that Yahweh does not need magicians or astrologers. In fact, He does not want us to become involved with magic, divination, witchcraft, astrology or other such practices.

He tells us that *He* is to be our source of wisdom and we need to rely upon Him. We should not turn to the stars for wisdom. And we should not look at the shape of a llama's kidneys, the fall of a pair of dice, the draw of a card, or any other such things to find out what He wants us to know. (See Leviticus 19:26; Deuteronomy 18:10-15; etc.)

He tells us in Deuteronomy 29:29 that He keeps certain things hidden from us, but He reveals everything we need to know in order for us to "follow all the words of [His] law."

The Bible says that Christians are "a royal priesthood . . ., that [we] may proclaim the excellencies of Him who has called [us] out of darkness into His marvelous light" (1 Peter 2:9). But we do not become part of this royal priesthood by being born into a Christian family. Each person has to make his or her own decision to believe in Jesus for salvation (see John 1:12).

Gods

Like the Incans and the Aztecs, the Mayans also had lots of gods. They believed in one god who was above all the others—Hunab Ku. But Hunab Ku was so hard to know and so far away that no one even cared about him.

The most important gods to the Mayans were the gods who seemed to make a difference in everyday life. The Mayans worshiped *Chac* (Chock), the rain-god; *Yam Kax* (Yahm Kahsh), the maize-god;

Chac, the rain god

and *Ix Chel* (Eesh Chell), the moon-goddess. Ix Chel was responsible for floods, weaving, medicine, and people's ability to have children.

The Mayans had gods for almost every activity you could think of. One list includes 166 different gods: a war-god, a wind-god, a sun-god, a god of death, a god of suicide, a god of poetry, gods for music, human sacrifice, trade, farming. . . . The list is almost endless.

The Mayan gods were not righteous. And they did not care about how people behaved. Whether people did good or bad, right or wrong, it didn't matter. What mattered was whether they offered the right sacrifices and whether or not they carried out the religious ceremonies and rituals in just the right way.[b]

Questions

- Did the Mayans have a few gods, many gods, or just one god?
- Were the Mayan gods concerned that people did right? If so, how did they express their concern? If not, what were the gods concerned about?
- How were the Mayan gods' concerns similar to Yahweh's concerns? How were they different?

Worship

The Mayans worshiped by praying, chanting, dancing, burning incense, and offering other sacrifices. The type of incense they burned was called *pom*. Pom is a very fragrant resin that comes from the copal tree.

Sometimes when the Mayans worshiped their gods, they also *let blood*. This means they stuck thorns or stingray spines through their ears, noses, lips, tongues, or other parts of their bodies. Then they smeared the blood onto their idols that came out of their bodies.

Most Mayan worship services ended with feasting and drinking until the people were drunk.

Sacrifices

Mayan sacrifices included food, ornaments, animals, pom, and human beings. Men were not the only victims. Sometimes

Wall carvings on Chac's temple

women were sacrificed. Children were also sacrificed. But the most common victims were prisoners of war.

The Mayans often sacrificed people in the same way that the Aztecs did (though not so many people at one time).

Victims were not always sacrificed on the stone altar at the top of a pyramid, however. Sometimes they were hanged, drowned, cut open, beheaded, or beaten to death. Occasionally they were tied to a stake, then had their hearts torn out. Sometimes they were thrown from the top of the pyramid before having their hearts removed. Occasionally they were shot full of arrows.

The Mayans often

Here, Shield Jaguar, Yaxchilan's ruler and high priest, holds a torch while his first wife, Lady Xoc, pulls a thorn-lined rope through her tongue.

made sacrifices in open caves called *cenotes* (say-NO-tays). Cenotes are very deep holes (70 feet deep or more), with water in them. Actually, they are limestone caves whose roofs have collapsed, making them open to the sky. There are many cenotes where the Mayans lived.

When someone was going to be thrown into a cenote, the priests and their helpers would spend 60 days getting ready. Then, at daybreak on the morning of the sacrifice, they would throw the person into the deep hole. But first, they gave the victim some instructions. They told the victim to ask the gods who lived under the water

Cenote

to bless the people. The Mayans did this because drought was a big problem. They needed water, and wanted the gods to send it.

Most people who were thrown into the cenotes never got out. But if they survived until noon, they would be dragged out and asked what the gods had said. There is a record of at least one man who survived being thrown into a cenote. He later became a great chief.

Questions
- What is *bloodletting*?
- What is a *cenote*?

☀☺☀☺☀☺☀☺☀☺☀☺☀☺☀☺☀

Today

The Incan and Aztec cultures were almost completely destroyed when the Spaniards arrived in the early 1500s. (We will read more about this later.) But this was not true of the Mayan culture. Many Mayan tribes still hold to their ancient traditions. Even many who now practice a form of Christianity have mixed it with the worship of false gods.[c]

Note For Adults:[c]

In 1959, in a cave a few miles from Chichen Itza, a part-time guide discovered a passageway sealed with stones. . . . The amateur explorer broke through the wall of tightly cemented stones and crawled through a narrow chamber into a maze of tunnels. At the end was a large cavern containing dozens of pottery vessels and other objects. When the discovery was reported, a team of archaeologists, photographers, and artists went to work in the cave for five weeks. . . . They recovered over six hundred artifacts. Some parts of the cave had been used as far back as 100 B.C.

> "The team had hardly begun work when a young Maya shaman, or native priest, came from a nearby village and explained that his people had known for generations of a secret place of prayer dedicated to the rain god . . . . But no one had been able to find this shrine. . . . When he saw the cavern, the shaman grew excited and asked permission to conduct special religious ceremonies there. He wanted to begin right away to placate [the rain god] and the balams, guardians of the cave and the water sources. These scientists had invaded their sacred area, and they were sure to be displeased.
>
> "The ceremonies began the next morning and continued for twenty-four hours. . . .
>
> "For perhaps a thousand years the cave had been all but forgotten . . . yet the young shaman somehow knew how his ancestors would have revered that shrine . . . using rituals he described as 'intended for use in chambers hidden beyond the memory of man.'
>
> "In spite of the efforts of missionaries to replace pagan beliefs with Christian faith, the Maya continue to mix the two, maintaining a strong emphasis on magic, witchcraft, and superstition.
>
> "The modern Maya . . . begs the favor of his ancestral gods before he plants his milpa [maize]—and attends mass on Sunday. . . ."
> —*Mysteries*, 146-148

Social Organization

Some of the Mayans lived where the country of Guatemala is today. Others lived just north of Guatemala, in the southeastern part of what is now called Mexico. This portion of Mexico is called the Yucatan peninsula.

Tikal (TEE-call) was a Mayan city in what is now Guatemala. The city covered more than 25 square miles. It had at least eight pyramids. One of the pyramids stands 229 feet high. Tikal also had many, many stelae, palaces,

At the spring and autumn equinoxes, a serpent-like "body" of light and shadow creeps down the stairway and joins the head of the Feathered Serpent carved in stone at the base of the steps. This is the main pyramid in Chichen Itza.

and altars. The city's grand plaza was about the size of two American football fields placed side by side. Yet in spite of its size, Tikal probably didn't have more than 50,000 people.

Another city, called *Uaxactun* (wah-HOCK-tun), was 35 miles away from Tikal. Uaxactun was just like Tikal, except a little smaller.

Archaeologists have studied these ancient cities and discovered that they were not like modern cities. They weren't designed for people to live in them. Instead, they were places for worship and for running the government.

The people themselves lived in small villages around the cities. An average village might include 15 to 20 households.

Within the village, the people would work together. They would help each other plant crops, harvest them, and build homes. But each family had its own plot of land.

Each village had an overlord who watched over it. The overlord directed the people in many of their tasks, and also collected taxes.

When the people paid their taxes, they didn't pay with money. They paid with food, animals, clothing, and things like that. A village of 20 households might pay its overlord 1,200 pounds of maize and 20 turkeys each year.

The people also had to work for the overlord. They had to work together to build houses, cultivate the fields of the overlord and of the priests, maintain the highways, and build temples, tombs, ball courts, reservoirs, and other such things. They also had to fight as warriors when necessary.

The peasants paid all the taxes and had to do all the manual labor. The nobles, priests, government workers, army officers, and merchants had much more freedom to do whatever they wanted.

The ruler who was above the overlords was called a *batab* (buh-TOB). He watched over a whole province. The villagers thought of the batab as a god. He had authority over everyone in the province.

When the batab came to a village and got out of his litter, the people spread their cloaks on the ground so he could walk on them. (They didn't want the "god" to have to touch the soil!)

When a Spanish captain went to speak to a batab, he had to speak through a cotton screen. No one was permitted to look at the batab.

The batab collected taxes from the overlords. When there was a major disagreement between people, the batab acted as judge. The batab told the people about "lucky" dates. And he told them when and where the gods wanted them to offer their sacrifices.

Questions

- Did the Mayans have cities? Explain your answer. *(They had areas that had massive structures similar to those we would find in a modern city, but they were not places in which people were meant to live. The cities were centers of government and religion.)*
- What was a *batab*?

Government

Leadership

If you want to speak of more than one batab, you say *batabob*. The batabob lived in the cities along with the other government and religious leaders.

Each city was independent of the others. It had its own chief. It had its own council. The chief inherited his role from his father. But the chief could choose the men he wanted on his council. One member of the council would serve as both the war chief and the chief priest. He would serve in these positions for three years. The council also included all the batabob, as well as important priests and other nobles.

The Mayan army was not like the Aztec army. The Aztec army was a *standing army*, which means the soldiers' only job was to be soldiers. The Mayans had no standing armies. Men would do their normal work, but be ready to fight if there was a war. This kind of army is called a *militia*.

Each village had its own militia under the command of a local leader. When there was a war, the village militias reported to the war chief.

Mayan men were well-trained for war. In fact, the Spaniards commented on how well-disciplined they were.

Criminal Justice System

The way the Mayans punished criminals was much different from the way criminals are punished in most Western countries today. The Mayans' punishments were closer to those we see in the Bible.

Stealing was considered disgraceful. If you stole something, you not only hurt the person from whom you stole, but you also disgraced your family. If you were caught, you didn't pay a fine to the government, and you weren't put in prison. Instead, you had to pay back the person from whom you had stolen. If you couldn't pay, you became your victim's temporary slave. If you were ever caught stealing a second time, you would be condemned to death.[2]

There are other ways of hurting a neighbor than directly stealing from him. For instance, suppose you borrowed your neighbor's hoe and while you were using it, it broke. Or suppose you happened to

---

[2] The idea that thieves should repay their victims for what they stole is something we find in the Bible (see, for instance, Exodus 22:1-15). The idea that a thief should be killed for stealing, however, is not found in the Bible.

trip over a stone, the stone popped out of the ground and hit your neighbor's water storage pot, and the pot broke. Then what happened? According to the Mayans, whether you meant to break your neighbor's things or not, if you broke them, you had to replace them![3]

Among the Mayans, if you killed someone, whether you meant to do it or not, you had to die. The Mayans believed that a person who killed someone acted under the power of an evil spirit. Whether he wanted to kill his victim or not, the evil spirit wanted to commit murder. So, since the murderer was under the control of an evil spirit, he had to die.[4]

Questions

- How were Mayan laws similar to those we find in the Bible?
- How were they different?

✺☺✺☺ ✺☺✺☺✺☺✺ ☺ ✺☺✺☺✺

Everyday Life

A Normal Day

For a Mayan peasant family, a typical day began between 4:30 and 5:30 in the morning.

The wife got up about this time to begin preparing the morning meal. She used a stone rolling pin to mash the maize that had been soaking overnight. The maize then formed a paste or dough that the woman used to make tortillas.

The husband also rose early in order to pray. He'd take embers from the fire and drop incense on them to make a sweet-smelling

---

[3] This rule is very similar to what we find in the Bible (see Exodus 21:33-36; Numbers 5:6-8).

[4] This rule is not the same as what we find in the Bible. In the Bible, if you intended to kill someone, then you had to be killed. But if you killed them by accident, then God said you weren't guilty (see Exodus 21:12-14 and Deuteronomy 19:4-5).

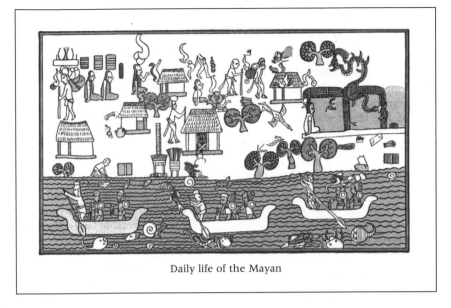

Daily life of the Mayan

smoke. As the incense burned, he would pray for good hunting, weather, or whatever else he felt he needed.

After prayer, the man ate beans, using a tortilla as a spoon. If he was going hunting, his wife would prepare him some maize dumplings, wrapped in a leaf, that he could take with him. If he was going to work in the field, his wife would bring his midday meal to him when the time came.

The Mayans ate their dinner at about 5 in the evening. Right before dinnertime was bathtime. They used wooden bathtubs, and usually preferred hot baths.

For dinner, the Mayans would eat tortillas with a stew made of meat, fish or eggs, plus herbs, vegetables, and fruit. For their drink, they would have either foaming chocolate or a honey drink. Foaming chocolate was made with cacao beans and maize flour mixed in water. The honey drink was made with honey and maize flour mixed in water.

After dinner, from about 5:30 until 8 or 9 at night, the men and women would work on crafts or sit and talk with their neighbors. The men might repair tools. The women would spin and weave or make things to be sold at market.

At about 8 or 9 at night, everyone would quit work to enjoy a light meal. This was similar to breakfast. Before they went to bed, the women would put more maize in lime water for the next day. They would then go to bed sometime between 8:30 and 9:30 at night.

Question
• Describe a typical day's schedule for a Mayan peasant.

🌟☺🌟☺ 🌟☺🌟☺🌟☺🌟 ☺ 🌟☺🌟☺🌟

A Typical Year
Each family had a plot of ground where they grew their maize. The plot for one family would be about 400 square feet in size. (That would be like a square that is 20 feet on each side.)

The Mayans did not have to work hard to get the food they needed. They spent only about two months of the year cultivating their maize.

They spent the rest of the year making crafts (like pottery, jewelry, weapons, and tools), building pyramids, hunting, going to war, or enjoying the festivals.

Major Events in a Person's Life
Birth
Among the Mayans, as soon as a baby was born, they would pray for the child. While they were praying, they would sprinkle a little of the blood from the birth on an ear of maize. The parents saved this special ear of maize for the next growing season. They would plant its kernels in a special plot of ground just for the child.

When the first year's crop was harvested, all the grain from the special plot was saved as seed to be planted again the next season. After the second season, there was usually enough maize to give a gift to the priests, to feed the child, and to save as seed for the following year. From that point on, the child had to live off the produce of that grain.

Besides the maize ceremony, there were other things that the Mayans did when a baby was born. The baby's mother would tie cords around his wrists and ankles so his soul wouldn't "escape."

A few days after a baby was born, his parents would strap his head in a special frame. The purpose of the frame was to make the baby's head longer. (The shape of a baby's head is not completely formed when the baby

Mayan home

is born. So if there is more pressure on one part of his head than another, it will affect the shape of his head.) The Mayans thought that a long head was very beautiful.

They also thought that squinty eyes were beautiful. So the parents would hang a ball of wax right in front of the baby. The ball of wax was right between the baby's eyes, so he had to squint to look at it.

A few weeks after a baby was born, the parents would pierce the baby's nose, lips, and earlobes. Then they could put ornaments in these holes.

Question
• What did Mayan parents do when a baby was born?

☀☺☀☺☀☺☀☺☀☺☀☺☀☺☀☺☀

The Hetzmek
A few months after a baby was born, its parents held a special ceremony called the *hetzmek* (HETZ-mek). When a hetzmek was held, the baby became a member of the community. For baby girls, the

hetzmek took place when they were three months old. For baby boys, it occurred when they were four months old.[5]

Before the hetzmek, the baby's parents asked two of their friends to be godparents to their child. These friends then came to the parents' hut for the hetzmek.

At the hetzmek, nine tools were placed on a mat in the center of the hut. For a boy, the tools included a hoe, a dibbing-stick for digging holes,[6] and other tools. For a girl, the tools included a *metate* (meh-TAH-tay) for grinding maize, a spindle for spinning yarn, a tiny loom for weaving cloth, a bit of cotton, a water jug, a cooking pot, and other such tools.

Once the tools were on the mat, the baby was set on the hip of one of the godparents. The godparent then walked around the mat and placed one of the tools in the baby's hand. The godparent explained to the baby how he or she would use the tool someday. Then the godparent put the tool down, walked around the mat again, and placed another tool in the baby's hand. This was done nine times, so the baby had a chance to see and feel each of the nine tools.

Questions
- Describe a *hetzmek*.
- Why were hetzmeks held when baby girls were three months old but when baby boys were four months old?
- Is the hetzmek similar to any ceremonies you're familiar with? If so, in what ways is it similar? How is it different?

🌞😊🌞☺🌞☺🌞☺🌞😊🌞☺🌞☺🌞😊🌞

Names
It was only after the hetzmek that the baby was named. Every Mayan had four names:

---

[5] Three was the "sacred number" for women. That's because the hearth had three stones and the hearth was the symbol of a woman's work in the home. Four was the "sacred number" for men because the field where the man worked had four corners.
[6] A dibbing-stick was used by the Mayans and the Aztecs to dig holes for planting maize and other vegetable seeds. It had a fire-hardened tip.

First, they had a personal name. This name was almost never used. It was thought to have almost magical powers. The only people who knew this name were the child and his or her immediate family.

The second and third names were two family names. One came from the father and one from the mother. To the Mayans, both the father's line and the mother's line were important—but in different ways. A family's inheritance came through the father. Marriages, however, were either allowed or not allowed based on the mother's name.

A man and woman could not marry each other if their mothers had the same family name. Even if the mothers were totally unrelated, but just happened to have the same family name, the man and woman could not get married. However, if it was the fathers who had the same family name, then the couple could get married. Even if the man and woman were first cousins on their fathers' sides, they could still marry each other.

Female Mayan: notice how the forehead slants back away from the nose, that's because of the elongation process where parents shaped the baby's head with a board.

The fourth name was a nickname. This was the name that everyone used all the time.

Male-Female Relationships

Mayan men and women treated each other very differently than people in our culture do. Men and women didn't do much together. In fact, they rarely spoke to one another. They acted almost as if they lived in different worlds.

If a woman met a man on the street, she always looked down, turned her back and stepped aside. The man always had the "right of way."

Husbands and wives never ate together. They could not laugh or have long conversations with one another.

When the Mayans danced, the men and women normally danced separately. A husband and wife could only dance together on rare occasions, at special festivals.

When a young man turned 14, he had to paint himself black. This would let everyone know that he was not married. He then had to move out of his parents' home to live in a house with other young men. There he learned crafts, studied warfare, and played games.

Questions

• Describe how men and women treated each other in Mayan society.
• How do men and women treat each other in your society?
• Is the way men and women treat each other in your society similar or different from the way they treated each other in Mayan society? In what ways?

☀☺☀☺☀☺☀☺☀☺☀☺☀☺☀☺☀

Marriage

Mayans got married at a much earlier age than most people in our culture do. Boys got married when they were about 18. Girls were usually married by the time they were 14. Mayan peasants married only one husband or wife, but the noblemen were allowed to have many wives.

Weddings among the Mayans were very similar to weddings among the Aztecs. A young man's parents hired a matchmaker. The matchmaker would find out which young women were ready to marry. Then the matchmaker would use astrology to find out if any of the young women would be a good match for the young man.

Once she had found what she thought was a good match, she discussed payment with the families. She helped them agree on the bride price. The bride price was what the young man's family would have to pay to the girl's family. The families would agree on how much cotton, how much tobacco, how much pom, how many cacao beans, etc. that the young man's family would pay.[7]

The matchmaker also helped the families decide how long the groom would have to work for his future father-in-law. Usually he would have to work from three to six years.[8]

After all these things had been decided, the matchmaker used divination to decide on the best day to hold the wedding.

The bride's parents then invited their friends and relatives to help build a hut for the couple and to furnish their home.

At the wedding ceremony itself, everyone gathered in the new hut. The priest lit incense and a fire in the hearth. He said some prayers over the couple, and he blessed them. Then he told everyone what the bride price was and how long the bridegroom would have to work for the bride's father.

After the priest was finished, the families exchanged gifts. A large feast and wild party was then held at the home of the bride's parents.

Male Mayan

All the guests at the wedding were invited to the party. The new couple, however, stayed at their home, sat in silence, and looked at the fire until it went out. They had no honeymoon. The next day they went back to work.

---

[7] Notice how this differs from Aztec society! Who paid whom in Aztec society? (See pages 93-94.) Who pays whom in your society? What about in Bible times?

[8] Remember Jacob and how he worked for Laban? See Genesis 29:15ff.

Questions

- How was marriage in Mayan society similar to marriage in your society?
- How was it different?

🌞☺🌞☺🌞☺🌞☺🌞☺🌞☺🌞☺🌞☺🌞

Death

In the Bible we are taught that when we die, those of us who love Jesus go to be with Him in heaven. Those who have refused to follow after Him go to a place that we call hell where there will be great suffering and "weeping and gnashing of teeth."[9]

The Mayans believed that when people died, the place they went depended on what social class they had belonged to on earth. They believed that there were thirteen upper-worlds and nine under-worlds. A certain kind of priest would go to a particular upper-world. A batab would go to another. A chief went to still another.

It didn't matter how good or bad anyone was. The upper- and under-worlds were not thought of as rewards or punishments. They were simply different kinds of

Palace of Palenque where the Mayan lord, Pacal, was buried

worlds. As far as the Mayans were concerned, life after death was pretty much the same as life before death.

The Mayans buried their dead with jade or other valuable objects in their mouths. They thought the person who died could use these

---

[9] Matthew 8:12; 13:42; Mark 9:47-48.

136

objects as money in the next world. They also buried pots of food, drink, tools, and other possessions that the person might need.

If the person had been rich, the Mayans would also bury a favorite dog, as well as the person's slaves, and the slaves' tools. They wanted the dead person to have these in the next world.

When someone died, those who were left "wept the day in silence, and at night they wailed."

Questions

- Can you think of any other cultures that treated (or treat) their dead in a manner similar to the way the Mayans treated theirs?
- Since slaves had to be buried with their masters when their masters died, what does that tell you about the Mayans' attitude toward the master? What does it tell you about their attitude toward the slaves? Were the Mayans' attitudes in these matters similar to the attitudes we are taught to have in Scripture? Why or why not? (See Galatians 3:26-28; Ephesians 6:5-9; Colossians 3:22-4:1; James 2:5.)

Culture

As we have already seen, each of the Mayan "cities" was independent of the others. There was no leading city like there was among the Aztecs. There was no strong leader among the Mayans like there was among the Incans.

Still, the Mayan people felt close to one another. They felt like they belonged together. They all had the same religion, the same language, and the same culture. They ate the same foods and produced the same kinds of artwork. They were one people group.

Food

The Mayans ate tortillas made from maize. It was their main food, just like it was for the Aztecs.

The Mayans also enjoyed honey. They especially enjoyed it because it came from stingless bees!

They ate fish, too. But they didn't use fishing poles to catch their fish. Instead, they drugged the fish, and then caught them by hand.

Arts & Crafts

The Mayans were very artistic people and used many different materials to make their crafts and works of art.

Earthworks

The Mayans' pottery was excellent. Many artists have remarked on how well-formed the pottery is, even though the Mayans did not have pottery wheels.

What did the Mayans make out of pottery? They made practical things like kitchen utensils, water jars, incense burners, and drain-pipes. And they made artistic things like figurines. The Mayans often painted their pottery. Black, red, orange, and grey were their favorite colors.

Just before the Spanish arrived, the Mayans had figured out how to glaze their pottery. This made their work even more durable . . . and beautiful.

Besides pottery, the Mayans also made plaster. Their plaster was a fine, shining material, and they put it all over their pyramids.

Then there was

Carved stone jaguar

stucco. The stucco was made out of clay, and it was thicker than plaster. The Mayans used stucco to make masks up to eight feet tall. They used stucco to add special artistic touches to pottery, and they also put it on their walls.

Carving of Mayan Glyphs

The Mayans made all kinds of sculptures. One type was basically flat but with figures that were raised up a little bit from the flat background. This type of sculpture is called *bas relief*.

Almost all Mayan sculptures were painted, and they were painted in vivid colors.

The Mayans also told stories in stone. They did this by carving glyphs into the stone. Another word to describe this is *hieroglyphs* (or hieroglyphics) which means "sacred carvings." The hieroglyphs told stories that the Mayans wanted to remember.

Sometimes stones with carvings on them were set on end. These were the stelae. Stelae are memorial stones set on end. The reason the stones were *memorial* stones is that they had something carved into them so it could be remembered.

Some of the Mayan stelae were 30 feet high.

One of the Mayans' most astonishing crafts was small jade statuettes. Jade is a certain kind of stone that is found in different shades of brown and green. It is an extremely hard stone. It's a wonder the Mayans could shape it.

But statuettes were not the only things the Mayans made out of jade. They also made *mosaics* using jade, iron pyrite, and turquoise. A mosaic is a picture or design made from little pieces of colored stone or other materials. The pieces are fitted together—kind of like a puzzle—to create the picture or design.

Carving of Pecate, the god of fishing

Questions
- What is *glaze*?
- What is *stucco*?
- What are *hieroglyphs* (or *hieroglyphics*)?
- What is a *mosaic*?

🌞☺🌞☺🌞☺🌞☺🌞☺🌞☺🌞☺🌞☺🌞

Metalworks

The Mayans bought their copper and gold from people groups in other areas. Usually they didn't just buy a chunk of copper or gold, but they bought something that was made out of copper or gold. So the Mayans themselves didn't make many things out of these two metals.

The Mayans did, however, work with iron pyrite. They used iron pyrite to make beads, mirrors, and tooth caps. Iron pyrite is also called *fool's gold* because it's shiny and yellow and people who find it sometimes think it's gold.

Other Materials

The Mayans used a lot of materials from the sea. They used pearls and coral to make jewelry. They used seashells to make beads and earplugs ("earrings"). They used large seashells, called *conches*, to make trumpets and rattles. (Conches are the kind of shells people often use to "hear the ocean.")

Pearls, coral, and seashells also served as money.

Question

• What are some of the materials the Mayans used to make works of art?

Agriculture

When people get ready to plant crops, they often have to prepare the ground. Crops won't grow very well if the ground is too hard or if it doesn't have enough nutrients. And, of course, it would be hard to plant crops or harvest them if there were too many trees in the way.

The way the Mayans prepared their land for planting was by burning it. This method is known as "slash and burn."[10] The Mayans would clear their land by starting a fire. The fire would burn off whatever trees and shrubs were growing there. And the ashes made a good fertilizer.

After the land was cleared, the Mayans would make holes about four to five inches deep. They would drop several seeds in each hole,

---

[10] The "slash and burn" method has been used by people groups in other parts of the world as well.

then cover them up. To make the holes, they used *dibbing-sticks*, just like the Aztecs did. A dibbing-stick was a special tool with a fire-hardened tip.

Some of the crops the Mayans grew included maize (of course), beans, sweet potatoes, squash, cacao, and cotton. The Mayans would trade cacao and cotton for other things they needed.

They also grew certain trees such as the copal tree. That's where they got the fragrant resin called *pom*. The Mayans used pom for incense, rubber, and chewing gum. They used incense for worshiping their gods. They used rubber for making rubber balls, and they used chewing gum . . . well, the same way we use it.

Question
• What is a *dibbing-stick*?

🌞☺🌞☺🌞☺🌞☺🌞☺🌞☺🌞☺🌞☺🌞

Clothing

Men wore a band of material around their waist and between their legs. Some got to wear deerskin moccasins and a cloak thrown over their shoulders.

Women wore a decorated cloth with holes for the arms and head. The women also wore a lightweight slip or petticoat. When they were not busy working, they would also wear a long piece of cloth over their shoulders.

When it was cold outside, both men and women wore a *manta*, a heavy, square piece of cloth. They also used the manta as a blanket at night.

Question
• What is a *manta*?

🌞☺🌞☺🌞☺🌞☺🌞☺🌞☺🌞☺🌞

Fashion

It is easy to think that tribal peoples couldn't possibly have the time to worry about fashions. Besides, without department stores, how could they have anything fashionable anyway? The Mayans didn't have department stores, but they certainly had fashions.

One of the easiest things they did to make themselves more fashionable was to work feathers into their clothing. Wealthy Mayans wore great feather headdresses. They used feathers as decorations on their cloaks. They made gorgeous feather fans. And they put feathers in banners.

The *best* kind of feathers were from birds called *quetzals* (KEH-tsals). The male quetzal has spectacular green and blue feathers. The very long tail feathers have some white underneath, and the bird's belly is red. Quetzal feathers were so valuable that if a Mayan killed a quetzal without having the right kind of license, he or she was punished by being put to death.

Besides quetzals, the Mayans also used the feathers of other kinds of beautiful birds.

Jewelry

Most Mayans wore jewelry made of bone, shell, wood, or stone. Those who had more authority in Mayan society were allowed to wear metal or jade ornaments. They placed these in their ears, in their noses, and in their lips.

Body Art

I had never thought of it as art, but one day it struck me: people in almost every culture do things to their bodies to make them more beautiful. In modern-day America, women wear cosmetics on their faces. Most of us get our hair cut in different ways. Some men and women get tattoos. Others put on special clothing that makes them look taller or thinner. In recent years, a lot of women wear fake fingernails.

The Mayans did many things to make themselves look prettier or more handsome.

Hair

Both men and women wore braids. They would wear either two or four braids. These braids were sometimes wrapped around the neck and sometimes allowed to hang straight down the back. Both men and women had bangs cut straight across their foreheads.

Teeth

A lot of Mayans filed their teeth into points. Then, to be extra fancy, they would cover them with caps made of obsidian or iron pyrite. Chiefs were allowed to wear tooth caps made of jade.

Body

The Mayans often tattooed themselves. And they painted themselves, too. Warriors painted themselves red and black. Priests painted themselves blue. Young people painted themselves black. And slaves were painted with black and white stripes.

Anyone who was cross-eyed or squinty-eyed was considered especially beautiful. Parents tried to make their baby cross-eyed or squinty-eyed by hanging a ball of wax between the baby's eyes, as discussed earlier.

The Mayans also thought that having a pointed head was pretty. So, as also previously mentioned, parents bound their babies' heads so they would become long and narrow.

The Mayans thought that long noses were pretty, too. So people would apply special clays to the tops of their noses to make them look like they extended up into their foreheads.

The upper classes and noblemen tried hardest of all to be fashionable. The chief's head was shaped to a true point. He wore jade coverings on his teeth. He wore huge earrings. His face and body were tattooed. His nose was made to look even straighter and longer than other people's noses. And he wore huge headdresses—sometimes even bigger than the chief himself.

Questions

- Name at least three ways people around the world try to make themselves look more attractive (e.g., special clothing, jewelry, body art).

- What is a *cosmetic*?
- What are some forms of body art that the Mayans used?
- Can you think of any forms of body art used in your culture?

🌞😊🌞😊🌞😊🌞😊🌞😊🌞😊🌞😊🌞😊🌞

Commerce

Commerce is the trading activity of a society. It involves trade between people within the society. And it also involves trade between these people and the people of other societies.

The Mayans did more trading than either the Incans or the Aztecs. Maybe it was because they didn't have to spend as much time as the Incans did in cultivating their garden plots. Or maybe it was because they didn't have to spend as much time as the Aztecs did in fighting wars. We don't know, but they certainly did a lot of trading.

Markets

The Mayans had market day about once every five days. People would bring what they had to sell, and come for what they needed to buy. At a Mayan market you would find fruits, vegetables, fish, deer meat, bird meat, cloth, feathers, tools, weapons, and more. Everything had its own place in the market.

Money

It was mentioned earlier that the Mayans used coral, pearls, and seashells as money. They also used cacao beans as money. In fact, the cacao bean was their most common form of money.

You would think it would be impossible to counterfeit a cacao bean. But counterfeiting was actually a common crime. Counterfeiters would carefully take off the husks of the cacao beans. They would use the beans for cocoa (chocolate powder), they would fill the husks with sand, and then they would mix those sand-filled husks with real beans.

Smart traders would always squeeze the beans first to make sure they were good.

Question

• How did some Mayans counterfeit their money?

✹☺✹☺✹☺✹☺✹☺✹☺✹☺✹☺✹

Trade

Trade could take place between any two people, but there were certain people in Mayan society whose job it was to trade.

These traders didn't just trade with people in their own towns. They traveled great distances to do their trading. They went by sea, by river, and by road. They traveled as far as Mexico to the north and modern-day Panama to the south. Traders were highly respected in Mayan society. They didn't have to pay taxes like the common people did.

The Mayans didn't have any animals to carry heavy loads for them. They didn't have llamas like the Incans did. They didn't have camels like some Asians and North Africans did. And they didn't have horses like the Spaniards did. They didn't have buggies or wagons either, because they hadn't developed the wheel. So Mayan traders (or their slaves) carried everything on their backs, in spite of the long distances they had to travel.

Salt, cotton, fabric made out of cotton, clothing, hammocks, honey, dried fish, seashells, and animal skins were just a few of the goods that the Mayans used for trading.

Some of the goods that they liked to receive in exchange were obsidian, jade, quetzal feathers, copal, and cacao beans.

Question

• How was trading different among the Mayans than it was among the Incans or the Aztecs?

✹☺✹☺✹☺✹☺✹☺✹☺✹☺✹☺✹

Slavery

In Mayan society, once a person became a slave, he could be a slave for the rest of his life. Most slaves came from poor families. If a family was poor, the parents might sell their children to make money. Other slaves were orphans. Still others were prisoners of war.[11] A person could also be born as a slave and be a slave for his or her entire life.

Slaves did the hard work. They carried heavy loads and paddled canoes. They often ground maize for richer people. And, while the rich owners rested, slaves fanned the flies away.

As was mentioned before, when a rich person died, his slaves were often killed and then buried with him.

Warfare

It seems that the Mayans didn't fight nearly as much as the Incans or the Aztecs. Maybe this was because there weren't as many other people around them. Maybe it was because trading was very important to them. People aren't likely to want to trade with you if, every time they see you coming, they think, "Oh, no! Run for your life!"

But probably the most important reason that the Mayans did not fight as much was the *way* they fought.

How the Mayans Fought

In a war, every Mayan man who was able to fight had to fight. And all the Mayan wives had to go along with their husbands to prepare food for them. That meant the

Warrior in costume

---

[11] If a prisoner of war had been an important person in his own society, he would be sacrificed to the gods. If he had been a commoner, he would become a slave of the Mayans.

women also had to carry the food that they were going to prepare for their husbands.

Since the women had to come along to feed their husbands, the battles couldn't be too far from home. The women had to take care of their children, too. Besides, can you imagine having to haul food hundreds of miles from home?

Mayan battles were very short. The Mayans considered food to be more important than war. Their battles always ended at nightfall so the soldiers could eat. And the Mayans didn't go to war during growing season. They waited until after the crops were grown and harvested.

Question

• What are some of the reasons the Mayans didn't go to war as much as the Incans or Aztecs did?

Weapons

The Mayans used clubs, daggers, slingshots, and spears. They had one kind of spear that had three points. It was made from carved seashell.

In the 900s (during the Classic Period), the Mayans also started using spear throwers (atl-atls—see picture on pg. 88), as well as bows and arrows. Also, at this time, they began using the same type of armor and shields that the Aztecs did.

The Purpose of Warfare

The Mayans' reason for going to war was the same as the Aztecs. They wanted to capture prisoners.

If one side captured the high priest/commander of the other side, that was the end of the war. The victorious army would bring the conquered high priest home to be sacrificed. They sacrificed the other officers and nobles as well. The common peasants who had been captured were kept as slaves.

Strategy

The Mayans had a battle strategy that was different from the Incans and the Aztecs. The Mayans would attack the enemy by surprise. When they decided to attack, they would blow whistles and trumpets, beat drums, and shout war cries. Then they would charge. They would throw spears and sling stones. As soon as those weapons were gone, they would fight in hand-to-hand combat.

Questions

- Describe how the Mayans' style of warfare was similar to the other peoples we have studied.
- Describe how it was different.

❀☺❀☺ ❀☺❀☺❀☺❀☺ ❀☺ ❀☺❀

Technology

In many ways, the Mayans were much more technologically advanced than the Incans or the Aztecs.

Mathematics

In mathematics, the Mayans were way ahead of the Incans and the Aztecs. And they were also way ahead of the Europeans.

The Mayans had a concept of place value (similar to our places for ones, tens, hundreds, etc.). They also understood the idea of zero.

In Europe at that time, people used the Roman numeral system. So they didn't have place value or "zero" until the Arabs introduced the Arabic numeral system in about the year 1000.

Our numeral system is what mathematicians call a *decimal* system. It is based on the number *ten*. The digit on the left has a value ten times what it would have if it were in the place immediately to the right. (100 is ten times greater than 10.) And that digit has a value that is ten times greater than what it would have if it was one more place to the right. (10 is ten times greater than 1.)

Hieroglyphic numerals

The Mayans' numeral system was a *vigesimal* system. It was based on the number *twenty*. And the Mayans wrote their numbers from top to bottom instead of from left to right. Each place was worth twenty times the one below.

So, instead of a ones' place, a tens' place, a hundreds' place, and so forth, the Mayans had a ones' row (on the bottom), then a twenties' row (next one up), then a four-hundreds' row, an eight-thousands' row, a one-hundred-and-sixty-thousands' row, and so forth. Each "numeral" had a value that was twenty times greater than what it would have if it was one row lower.

However, the Mayans didn't use the numerals "1," "2," and "3," like we do. Instead, they used dots and bars. A dot stood for one, and a bar stood for five. A dot and bar together stood for six. A bar and two dots meant seven, etc. (See the diagram on next page.)

For zero, the Mayans used a symbol that looked like a coffee bean.

Astronomy

There is a big difference between *astrology* and *astronomy*. *Astrology* has to do with the supposedly "lucky" and "unlucky" location of stars and planets in the sky. *Astronomy* is a type of science. It has to do with studying what the stars are made of, how they move, and things like that.

The Mayan priests believed in astrology. That was part of the reason why they also wanted to study astronomy.

The Mayans measured how long it takes for the moon to go around the earth (the lunar month). They figured the lunar month was 29.5302 days (29 days, 12 hours, 43 minutes, and 46 seconds).

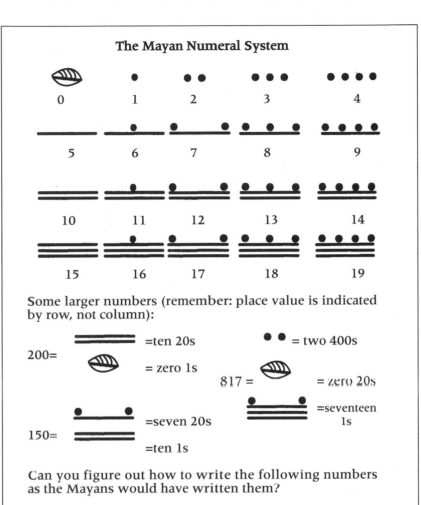

The Mayan Numeral System

Some larger numbers (remember: place value is indicated by row, not column):

200= =ten 20s / = zero 1s

150= =seven 20s / =ten 1s

817 = = two 400s / = zero 20s / =seventeen 1s

Can you figure out how to write the following numbers as the Mayans would have written them?

378   517   6,248   73   197,214

Modern astronomers, using all the most advanced scientific equipment, figure the lunar month is 29.53059 days (29 days, 12 hours, 44 minutes, and 20 seconds). That's a difference of only thirty-four seconds.

The Mayans also measured how long it takes for Venus to go around the sun (the Venusian year). They figured it was close to 584 days.

Modern astronomers figure the Venusian year is 583.92 days. That's pretty close—about two hours' difference out of a year and a half.

The Mayans figured these things out long before the "modern astronomers" did.

Civil Engineering

The Mayans were not quite as advanced as the Incans when it came to building bridges, roads, or aqueducts. But they didn't have to be. Their land wasn't as difficult as the areas where the Incans lived.

The Mayans did have some interesting roads, though. Some of their roads were "white roads." The white roads were from twelve to thirty-two feet wide and were raised up several feet off the ground. They were made of cement over stones. The longest white road modern explorers have discovered is sixty-two miles long.

Architecture

The Mayans' homes were very simple. They were either square or rectangular. There were two parts to a house—a kitchen and a sleeping area. A wall or a screen separated the two parts.

In the lowlands, the houses were usually built of wood. The foundations were made of stone and the roofs were made of palm leaves.

In the highlands, the houses were built with stone walls and grass roofs. The roofs were always steep so the heavy rains would run off.

A Mayan kitchen had a stone hearth in the center. That's where the woman would do her cooking. There was no chimney

Mayan arch

so the smoke collected in the room. Eventually it would go up through the roof or out the doorway, but it made it hard for people to breathe. The good part was that the smoke heated the house.

The Mayans had wooden tables and wooden stools.

Mayan houses had doorways but no doors. To create privacy and

Carved wall at a temple

keep the cold out, they might place a blanket or some other cloth over the doorway. Most houses had a string of bells on the front, by the entrance. If someone came to the entrance, they would jingle the bells.

When a couple got married, they lived in a small hut. As was already mentioned, this hut was given to the couple by the wife's parents. The hut was just a temporary house. The couple would live there while the husband worked for his wife's parents.

After the husband had completed his time of working for his in-laws, the whole community built the young family a larger house.

When members of a family died, they were always buried under the floor. When the father and mother had both died, everyone else moved out of the house. The abandoned house then became a shrine in honor of the father and mother.

Like the Incans and the Aztecs, the Mayans also built pyramids. The largest Mayan pyramid is 288 feet high. This is about 70 feet taller than the Aztecs' Pyramid of the Sun.

Medicine

The Mayans believed that illnesses were not natural. They believed that if someone was sick, it was either because the gods had made them get sick, or it was a punishment for sin, or the result of a curse. In order to be cured, they believed that a priest had to use divination to find the source of the sickness. Then the priest would have to offer the right kind of prayers and sacrifices, and prescribe the right medicines.

The Mayans believed that one of the best medicines was tobacco. They figured it was good for toothaches, snake bites, asthma, indigestion, headaches, head colds, and problems with childbirth. They also believed it could be useful in protecting them from witchcraft.

One cure that Mayan witch doctors often recommended was *bloodletting*—letting a person bleed. Doctors in Europe at that time often recommended the same thing.

Some of the more unusual medicines the Mayans used were a bat (the animal) dissolved in alcohol, a live toad dissolved in alcohol, woodpeckers' bills, and feathers. One prescription said, "If all else fails, have [the patient] remove one sandal, urinate in it and drink it."

Question

• What were some of the interesting things that the Mayans accomplished?

End of the Story

The Beginning of the End: 1492

It was A.D. 1492. The people of Europe were in a very difficult situation. It seemed to them that the world was coming to an end.

For centuries, Arab Muslims had controlled the Holy City, Jerusalem. The Muslims did not believe in Jesus as their Savior. They believed in Allah, and in Muhammad as the prophet of Allah.

The Christians thought Jerusalem should belong to Christians and not Muslims, but no matter how often they had attacked the Muslims, and no matter how large an army they had sent, they had been unable to move the Muslims out of Jerusalem.

It was bad enough that Muslims controlled Jerusalem. But then, in 1453, Muslim Turks had taken over Constantinople, the capital city of the Eastern Roman Empire. The Muslims had killed Emperor Constantine XI. And, when they killed him, they also killed the dreams of many people. The people had dreamed that Constantinople would always be a Christian city, but now this would not be true.

From 1453 on, the Muslim Turks had been on the attack. They conquered Athens in 1456. They took over Bosnia in 1463. They took Herzegovina in 1467. In 1492, the Turks invaded Hungary. They were marching toward Vienna.

Those Christians who refused to submit to the religion of Allah knew what to expect if the Muslims won. The Muslims would say that the Christians were disobedient to the will of God and the word of Muhammad His Prophet. They would call the Christians "infidels" (unfaithful ones). The Christians could expect either to have their heads cut off or to be sawn in two.

Most Christians were scared.

If you read a book called the *Nuremberg Chronicle*, you can understand how the people of Europe felt at that time. It is dated July 12, 1493, and it claims to be about "the events most worthy of notice from the beginning of the world to the calamity of our time." If you read this book, you can see that the people at that time really thought the end of the world was coming.

The only place in Europe where the people had hope was Spain. People in the rest of Europe worried about the Muslims coming to take over their cities. But the people in Spain had *already* been under Muslim control for almost 800 years. The Spaniards were actually gaining new strength and confidence.

You see, instead of giving in to the Muslim religion and way of life, Spain was becoming a distinctly *Christian* country.

España: A Christian Country

In 1469, Ferdinand of Aragon and Isabella of Castile married. Both of them were Catholic. They were devoted to Christ and they were devoted to the Church. Ten years after their marriage, in 1479, they had decided to bring their lands together to form what we know today as the country of Spain.

For a long time, other Europeans had made fun of the Christians in Aragon and Castile. The other Europeans called them "Moors." That was an insult. People who were called "Moors" were being told they were non-Christians, uncivilized rats: things worthy only of being killed.

In 1480, Ferdinand and Isabella decided to do something to stop their people from being called "Moors." They started what today is known as the Spanish Inquisition.

Up until that time, many Jews and Muslims in Spain had said that they had converted to Christianity. They had been baptized as Christians. But, their neighbors said, they continued to practice their old religions.

The purpose of the Spanish Inquisition was to "inquire," or ask, whether people who said they were Christians really believed the Christian faith. The Inquisition was meant to make sure that no pretend Christians would be permitted to remain in the Church. King Ferdinand and Queen Isabella declared that if a person claimed to be Christian, he or she had to be a full Christian. Those who only pretended to be Christians were not Christians at all.

Before this, Muslims, Jews, and Christians had lived side by side at peace in this kingdom for hundreds of years. But no longer would Muslims and Jews be tolerated. From that time forward, Muslims and Jews had to either renounce their faith or face the anger of the government.

In 1487, the Christian armies of Ferdinand and Isabella were able to defeat the Muslims who had ruled in the city of Malaga on the Iberian Peninsula.[1] On January 2, 1492, their armies overthrew the Muslim rulers in the city of Granada.

At that point, Spain became a "Christian" country, a country ruled by Christians. . . . And once they had achieved that goal, Ferdinand and Isabella were able to pay the money that it cost to send a sea captain out on a risky journey. The sea captain's name was Christopher Columbus.

Christopher Columbus

1492, as you know, was the year that Christopher Columbus sailed to America. Why did he set sail? He wanted to get to India. He knew that the Muslims controlled the land routes to India and China. But Columbus thought there might be another way to get there. And, if he could find this other way, perhaps he could find the money the Christians needed to attack the Muslims in Jerusalem.

Maybe the Christians could win Jerusalem back from the Muslims.

Columbus' journey never paid for an attack upon the Muslims in Jerusalem, but it did change the world.

Suddenly the Europeans—and especially the peoples of Spain and Portugal—began to look beyond Europe. They stopped looking only at themselves and thinking about how miserable they were. They saw a new world, a world to the west, a world of wealth and opportunity.

And while it was a world with great opportunities to become rich, it was a world, too, of heavy responsibilities. There were people already living in the west—people for whom Christ had died. And Christopher Columbus, "Admiral of the Ocean Sea," never forgot that his name, Christopher, meant "bearer of Christ." He was called to be a servant of the gospel.

---

[1] The Iberian Peninsula is the section of Europe that sticks out to the south and west. Spain and Portugal are both located there.

Questions

- What are some of the reasons Christopher Columbus sailed to the west and discovered the Americas?
- Why did he *not* sail until 1492?

☀☺☀☺☀☺☀☺☀☺☀☺☀☺☀☺☀

First Contact Between Europeans and the Mayans

Between 1492 and 1503, Columbus made four trips across the Atlantic Ocean. It was in 1502 that he first made contact with the Mayan Indians of Honduras.

Twenty-five Indians, packed into an open canoe . . . were making their way east towards the island of Guanaja [gwah-NAH-ha]. . . On board the boat, the Indian chief was sitting in the shade of a canopy surrounded by . . . men, women, and children. He was en route from the Yucatan to trade with the natives of the coast and islands. . .

Suddenly one of the men cried out in surprise. In all the time he had been sailing these waters he had never noticed the three great reefs off Guanaja. A moment later one of his companions gave an even louder cry; he thought he had seen one of the reefs move. Suddenly, the paddlers stopped stock still and exchanged worried glances. The chief silently gave the signal to continue. On the islands, which looked like large, half-submerged bowls, stood tall, bare tree trunks from which hung a network of ropes. The islands were obviously inhabited; human forms could be seen moving above the dark masses. Were they people or gods? All that could be seen of the creatures were their faces and hands, and their faces—the Indians soon discovered—were often covered with hair, like a monkey's.

Bravely, the expedition approached the floating mountains. At their summit the creatures began to point and talk in loud voices. Could these reefs be vast boats that the creatures had built themselves? Rope ladders were thrown down, and the Indians were invited to go aboard. The chief set an example by clambering up. Gifts were exchanged. There was amazement on both sides; they stared at each other, felt each other's clothes, skin, and ornaments. The strangers could not speak the Indians' language, so they pointed in the direction from which the canoe had come, and the Indians replied *maiam* [MY-am].

—From *Lost Cities of the Mayas*, 14-15.

This was the first contact between Mayans and Europeans. It would not be the last.

The Aztec Experience

S eventeen years after Columbus' first contact with the Mayans, a messenger from the Gulf of Mexico delivered his message to Montezuma.[2] It was early in the Aztec year of One Reed (A.D. 1519).

The messenger told Montezuma about a strange sight. Some of Montezuma's subjects had seen a hill that moved on water. Messengers who came later said the same thing—they had seen some floating towers. These towers carried men with yellow beards and faces as white as chalk. And the men owned deer that carried them wherever they wanted to go. The deer held the men as high as the roofs of houses.

Montezuma sent a few men to see whether these reports were true. Yes, the reports *were* true. . . . And there was more.

The strangers owned machines that shot balls of stone great distances. They shot these balls with such force that they could split a tree. And not only that, but when the machine threw a stone, it made a great noise. And it produced flames. And it created an awful smell.

---

[2] This reference to Montezuma, as well as those that follow, are referring to Montezuma II.

In the past, Montezuma had watched people in his kingdom shake with fear whenever he passed. Now, suddenly, it was *he* who was shaken.

Could this be the god Quetzalcoatl, who had said he would return in the year One Reed? Had Quetzalcoatl actually come back?

Montezuma didn't sleep very well. He had bad dreams and disturbing visions in the night. Were these strangers *men*? he wondered. . . . Or were they gods?

He decided to send them gifts—gifts of special clothing, food, drink . . . and gold. Lots of gold. More gold than the Spaniards (for that is who the strange visitors were) had ever seen before. There was a helmet packed with gold dust, golden figurines of birds and fish and seashells . . . and a disk of gold, and another of silver.

The Spaniards were amazed.

These Spanish *conquistadors* (con-KEES-tah-dores, meaning "conquerors") were not from great families. They were not wealthy. One of them, Francisco Pizzaro, had been herding pigs for a living when Columbus returned from America the first time. (Pizzaro was the man who would eventually overthrow the Incans.)

The conquistadors wondered: *Have we found the El Dorado—the very rich city that we have heard stories about?* According to the legend, El Dorado was filled with gold and full of opportunity.

We have already described the first meetings between the Aztecs and the conquistadors. Montezuma told his Aztec warriors, "If, by any chance, he [Cortés, but Montezuma wasn't sure if he was Quetzalcoatl]—. . . If . . . he does not like the food that you give him and . . . wishes to eat you, allow yourselves to be eaten . . . ."

The Aztec warriors followed Montezuma's command and went to the coast, not knowing what would happen there.

The Aztec warriors sacrificed a slave and sprinkled his blood on the meal they had prepared. But their visitors were obviously disgusted at the blood sacrifice. So the warriors prepared another meal, but without blood.

However, the fact that the Spaniards had been disgusted by the blood sacrifice made the Aztecs even more sure that the conquistadors were not men, but gods. And Cortés must be Quetzalcoatl. For they suddenly remembered what their magicians had told them— *Quetzalcoatl hated human sacrifice.*

Montezuma's warriors brought their report back to their leader. Montezuma then sent his men back with more gifts and more gold. He also told them to plead with the strangers to go back to the place from which they had come.

The warriors again did as Montezuma commanded, and went back to this person they thought was a god. "We give you these gifts in hopes you will be satisfied," said the warrior spokesmen. "We hope you will not be displeased with us. The road to our city is dangerous, and there isn't enough food in our city to provide for such a god as you. . . ."

But the Spaniards moved on toward Tenochtitlan. "If the Aztecs are trying so hard to send us away," they thought, "how much greater wealth must they be hiding?"

Montezuma tried whatever he could to keep the Spaniards away from Tenochtitlan. He sent sorcerers to cast spells on them. He sent guides to lead them by a dangerous path. But no matter what he did, the Spaniards kept moving on toward Tenochtitlan.

Questions
- Why was Montezuma afraid?
- Suppose you were one of the men with Cortés. Suppose you were Francisco Pizzaro. All you had ever done was care for pigs. Now suppose a king sends you lots and lots of gold and he asks you to go away. He seems scared. Do you think you would go? Or do you think you would try to scare him some more? Why?

The Fall of Tenochtitlan
On their way to Tenochtitlan, the Spaniards passed by the territory of the *Tlaxcalans* (tlash-CAH-lans). As we have already read, the Tlaxcalans were surrounded by the Aztecs. But they were never defeated by the Aztecs.

When the Spaniards passed by, the Tlaxcalans attacked them. After all, what did they have to lose? If they beat the Spaniards, the Spaniards wouldn't be able to help them or to hurt them in their battles with the Aztecs. But, if the Spaniards won, that would mean the Spaniards were good fighters. In that case, the Tlaxcalans could apologize for fighting against them, and see if they could fight *with* the Spaniards against the Aztecs.

At first, there were just small fights between the Tlaxcalans and the Spaniards. Then the Tlaxcalan chief sent hundreds of turkeys and baskets of tortillas to Cortés and his army. He said he wanted to fatten the Spaniards so they would make a decent meal. "Already," he said, "my women are boiling tomatoes and chili peppers."

The two sides got ready for a big battle.

The Tlaxcalans had an army of 50,000 warriors. There were less than 600 Spaniards. The night before the big battle, the Spaniards prayed. They confessed their sins to God and asked Him to let them survive.

Early the next morning, the battle began. It lasted for hours. One group of Indian warriors would attack, and the Spaniards would defeat them. Another group would attack, and the Spaniards would defeat them. And so it went. As more Indian warriors came up to fight, they had to walk on the bodies of the other Indians who had gone before them.

By nightfall, neither side had won. The Tlaxcalans didn't win, because they lost so many men. The Spaniards didn't win because they didn't have many men to begin with. But the fact that 50,000 warriors had not been able to defeat a few hundred Spaniards convinced the Tlaxcalans' chief to make peace.

From that point on, the Tlaxcalans and the Spaniards were allies. The Tlaxcalans provided food, workmen, and warriors to help the Spaniards.

The Aztec leaders didn't know whether they should welcome the Spaniards to their city or fight them. They still weren't quite sure whether these strangers were gods or men.

Finally they decided to fight. But then they didn't know *how* to fight the strangers. The Spaniards didn't use the same kinds of weapons that the Aztecs did. The Spaniards had guns. And guns were a lot better than spears and swords.

As was already mentioned, the Aztecs were used to fighting short battles. For the Aztecs, it only took one battle to figure out who won. But the Spanish were used to battling for days or weeks or months . . . or even years, if necessary.

The Aztecs were used to taking prisoners. But the Spanish idea of fighting was to kill enemy soldiers.

The Aztecs were used to going to war so they could capture more people to sacrifice to Huitzilopochtli. But the Spaniards wanted to *destroy* the whole religious system of the Indians. The Aztecs were certainly not used to that idea.

The Spaniards came to the New World to establish a new society, to destroy the pagan ways of the Indians, to get riches for their king, and to get rich themselves. (They did not necessarily hold these goals in this order.)

It would be hard for the Aztecs to defeat the Spaniards.

But the Spaniards only had four or five hundred men. The Aztecs had 200,000. The Spaniards knew they had to be very careful. If they were careless, they would be the Aztecs' next sacrificial victims.

It would be hard for the Spaniards to defeat the Aztecs.

The pressure was great—for both sides.

In the end, the conquistadors and their Indian allies surrounded Tenochtitlan and destroyed it completely. By the time they were finished, in August of 1521, not a single stone remained standing on another. About 240,000 Aztec people had died, and those that remained were just skin and bones. A once powerful empire was no more.[3]

Questions

• What made the warfare between the Spaniards and the Aztecs worse?
• What do you think could have made the warfare less deadly?

[3] The full story of how Tenochtitlan fell, what happened to the Spaniards, and what happened to the Aztecs is far too long to tell you here. If you'd like to learn more, I recommend a book called *Aztecs and Spaniards: Cortés and the Conquest of Mexico* by Albert Marrin (New York, NY: Atheneum, 1986).

The End of the Incan Empire

The Incan Empire was destroyed both from the inside and the outside.

Even before Francisco Pizzaro and his band of conquistadors arrived, there was trouble in the Incan Empire. Two sons of a High Inca fought each other over who should rule. One of the two, Atahualpa, eventually defeated the other, and became the next High Inca. But the fighting had badly weakened the Incan army—and the whole Incan Empire.

It wasn't until November of 1532 that the Spaniards and the Incans faced each other in battle. The Incans had the men, but the conquistadors had the weapons.

The conquistadors also had another advantage—surprise. Within half an hour, the conquistadors killed more than 2,000 Incan warriors. They also captured Atahualpa, the High Inca.

The conquistadors told Atahualpa that if his people would give enough treasures to the Spaniards, they would free him. The Incans gave the conquistadors what they asked for, but the conquistadors refused to release Atahualpa. Instead, they said he was guilty of arranging for the murder of his brother.

They told Atahualpa that they would do the same thing their government did to all non-Christian murderers—they would burn him to death. On the other hand, if he would confess faith in Christ, they would make his death less painful. They would strangle him instead. Atahualpa confessed faith in Christ. And the conquistadors strangled him.

The conquistadors in Peru were more unruly than those in Central America. Hernán Cortés up in Mexico had been able to keep his men under control. In Peru, it seems, every man looked out only for his own interests.

In fact, in Peru, different groups of Spaniards fought each other. Who would gain the wealth? Who would hold the power? They fought each other to find out. This fighting lasted for about eight and a half or nine years after the Incan Empire was defeated. In the meantime, the Incan people suffered greatly.

In 1548, the Spanish king was finally able to arrest the last Peruvian conquistador. The time of selfish rule had finally come to an end.

Question
- What did the conquistadors do to the Incans and to Atahualpa that was very wrong?

🌞☺🌞☺🌞☺🌞☺🌞☺🌞☺🌞☺🌞

What Happened to the Mayans?

No one really knows what happened to the Mayans. There were a number of battles between the Spaniards and the Mayans. But the Spaniards never gained control over the Mayans.

About three hundred years after Cortés first met the Mayans, some Western explorers found ancient cities that had been built by the Mayans. But what happened in those three hundred years? No one seems to know.

Most scholars assume that the modern-day Quechua Indians are the former Mayans.

A Balanced View of Spanish Rule

Most books about Central and South America make sure you hear about how bad the conquistadors were. When the conquistadors first came to power, they took large pieces of land from the Indians. They forced Indians to be slaves. Millions of Indians died as a result of the conquistadors' cruel treatment. The Spaniards forced the Indians to stop worshiping their idols, and introduced them to a form of Christian belief and practice.[4] In the case of the Aztecs, the conquistadors destroyed almost every book they had ever written.

---

[4] I say "a form" because the Indians wound up mixing a lot of Christian and non-Christian beliefs and practices together.

Many authors say it would have been better if Columbus had never come to America.

But just how bad—or good—was Spanish rule, really?

An author named Philip Powell says that, to be fair, we need to compare the way the Spaniards treated the Indians with the way other Europeans treated the Indians. If we do that, he says, we will be amazed.[5]

Powell says that, after Columbus discovered the Americas, Spanish leaders found themselves asking many questions. They had to try to answer questions that none of them had asked before. Here are some of the questions they had to ask:

1) Are Indians really human?
2) If so, how human are they?
3) Are Indians able to think the way Europeans can?
4) Do Indians have souls that need to be saved?
5) If the Indians are human and can be saved, what is the best way to bring them to the Lord? Should they simply be allowed to hear the gospel message and *choose* how they want to respond? Or is their culture so bad that they need to be *forced* to follow the Christian religion?
6) Is their culture so bad that they need to have Spaniards rule over them?
7) Would it be legal and maybe even a good thing to make slaves of them?

These were not—and, even today, are not—unfair questions. In England up until the late 1700s and early 1800s, sailors weren't even thought to have souls. Most pastors thought there was no hope for sailors; they could not be saved. A ship's captain could treat his crew however he wanted. He could be kind to them or he could be cruel to them; the judges in Britain didn't even care.

In the United States, judges and courts didn't recognize African slaves as fully human until sometime during the 1860s. A slave counted as only three-fifths of a man. He was the property of his owner, and the owner could sell him at any time.

---

[5] Philip Wayne Powell, *Tree of Hate* (New York, NY: Basic Books, 1971).

We must be careful how we judge others, for we, too, will be judged by the same standard.

Powell says there is another reason we should be careful how we judge what the Spaniards did in Central and South America. He points out that other European nations were envious of the Spanish. The English, Dutch, and French saw how Spain became rich from her land in the New World. These other countries looked for any excuse they could use to attack and steal from Spain.

So, if there was anything evil that the Spaniards did, the "opinion-makers" in England, Holland, and France tried to tell people about it. But when the Spaniards did good things for the Indians, the "opinion-makers" in these other countries made sure they said nothing. They wanted people to think Spain did more bad than good. They wanted people to think there was a good reason to attack Spain.

We have "opinion-makers" today, too. They are the ones who try to decide for the public what is "newsworthy" and what is not.

It is unwise to listen to only one side of a story. Most of us in North America have only been told the story as it was written by non-Spaniards. We should also listen to what the Spaniards say.

Powell gives a third reason why we should be careful when we study how the Spaniards treated the Indians. The Spaniards were debating their questions in public. The English, Dutch, and French leaders were struggling with the very same questions, but they didn't talk about them as much, so very few people ever heard about the arguments—what the English, Dutch, and French were doing right, and what they were doing wrong as well.

When we compare Spain with England, Holland, and France, "th[e Spanish] debate, . . . [w]as one of the glories of Spanish history," says Mr. Powell.[6] The Spaniards had great freedom of speech—freedom to say what they wanted. They could even criticize the king.

You wouldn't have found that kind of behavior in other European countries. In most European countries at that time, if you criticized the king, you were severely punished. You would at least be thrown in prison. You would probably be put to death.

Question

- Do you think there is any good reason to think that maybe the Spaniards were not as bad as a lot of people have said they were? Why or why not?

☀☺☀☺☀☺☀☺☀☺☀☺☀☺☀

The "New Laws of the Indies"

What was the result of the Spanish debate? In 1542, the king of Spain made a new set of laws. These laws were to be enforced in the Spanish colonies in the New World. (The Spanish called these lands the *Indies*.) The laws were called "New Laws of the Indies for the Good Treatment and Preservation of the Indians."

One of the new laws said that the Indians would not have to pay tribute to their Spanish conquerors.

As we have already seen, the idea of tribute was important to the Incans and the Aztecs. It is likely that it was also part of the Mayan way of life. The Spanish king *outlawed* the taking of tribute.

He also made it clear that it was against the law to make an Indian a slave.

The Spanish king not only made these laws, he also made sure they were enforced. It wasn't easy to enforce laws in lands so far away. But the king was willing to do whatever it took, and pay whatever it cost, to make sure these new laws were enforced.

In fact, the king was so strict about making sure his laws were followed that many Spanish colonists rose up in rebellion against him. He enforced the laws anyway. He did this at great cost to himself and to his government. He did it even though the Spanish colonists didn't like it. And he did it in *favor* of the Indians.

What "really" happened when the Spaniards came to power? We know that the native cultures were suppressed. This means that both good things and bad things soon disappeared. Good things like tech-

---

[6] Ibid., 30.

nological achievements were cut short. And bad things like human sacrifice ended.

For twenty years or so after the Spaniards arrived, there was bloodshed and misery. Indians died by the thousands.

The Spanish king (also called the Spanish Crown) was very concerned about the fact that so many Indians were dying. His concern could be seen in both the laws he made and the letters he wrote.

But it was not just the conquistadors who were to blame for the killing of Indians. As Powell says: "It is quite accurate to [say that] Spanish success in America [w]as a process of Indians conquering Indians, under white supervision. The American Indian was often more the conqueror of his own race than were the Spaniards."[7]

Today we call all the native peoples "Indians." It might seem that Indians should be loyal to other Indians. But as we have already seen, there were lots of different tribes and lots of different peoples in the Americas before the Spaniards came.

Just because they all lived in the Americas doesn't mean they all spoke the same language or had the same kind of lifestyle. Nor did it mean they liked each other or even refrained from killing each other. In fact, they often *did* kill each other.

Actually, says Powell, the Spanish governments in Central and South America were astonishingly good to the people whom they conquered. Gifts, honors, protection, privileges, and education were all given to the native peoples.

Powell gives some examples of the good things that the Spaniards did in Central and South America:

1. They ruled Central and South America for 300 years. And they did so without a standing army, except in a few places where there was danger of foreign attack. During all that time, "there was not a single rebellion that indicated widespread dissatisfaction with the Crown's rule."[8]

---

[7] Ibid., 20.
[8] Ibid., 28.

Powell says that if there had been great dissatisfaction, then the Spanish king would have needed an army to put down rebellion.[9]

2. Taxes in Spanish America were lower than in some parts of Spain itself.

3. Conditions in much (if not most) of Spanish America have been much worse since Spanish rule was overthrown.

4. There was greater peace in Spanish America than in most of Europe at that time.

5. "Lima, Peru, in colonial days had more hospitals than churches and averaged one hospital bed for every 101 people, a considerably better average than Los Angeles has today."[10]

6. Spaniards founded 23 colleges and universities in America. About 150,000 students graduated from these schools. By contrast, Portugal didn't found a single university in its South American colony Brazil.[11] And "the total of universities established by Belgium, England, Germany, France, and Italy during later . . . colonial periods . . . suffers by any fair comparison with the pioneering record of Spain."[12]

Question

• Do you think the Spaniards did anything right while they ruled in South America? If so, what? And why do you believe that?

[9] Compare this with the United States. One of the main reasons for the American Revolution was that the king of England wanted to have a standing army stay in the homes of American colonists.

[10] Dr. Francisco Guerra, Professor of Pharmacology at the University of Mexico, in University of California *Bulletin*, V, no. 28; quoted in Powell, 24-25.

[11] In fact, the Portuguese didn't found any universities in any of their lands overseas.

[12] Powell, 25. Note the use of the words "later" and "pioneering." One would normally expect a pioneer to have a harder time doing even as close to as good a job as one who comes after. Put another way: Spain, the pioneer, did a better job than England, Germany, France, and all the other nations that followed. The hard-working pioneer did better than all the countries that had the easier time following.

Conclusion

The Incans, Aztecs, and Mayans all had some remarkable cultural achievements.

The Incans built amazing roads. They also showed great skill in irrigation, farming, and stone-masonry.

The Aztecs reclaimed land from a swampy lake and grew crops on it. They built a huge city in the middle of the lake, and kept it very clean and well-ordered.

The Mayans had an incredible understanding of mathematics and astronomy.

In each case, modern scientists stand in awe of what these cultures achieved.

At the same time, from a Christian perspective, there were parts of these cultures that were very wrong. Their greatest and saddest error was their commitment to serve a created thing—the Sun—rather than to serve the Creator (see Romans 1:18-25). Their commitment to human sacrifice only made things worse. From Yahweh's perspective, their commitment to demons suited them for judgment , , , and they were judged when the Spanish came.

Those Incans, Aztecs, and Mayans who survived the initial destruction of their culture were also blessed. They were freed from the bondage of human sacrifice. And they were freed from the fear of almost constant war.

Today, the Gospel of Jesus Christ is going forward in Central and South America as it has never gone forward before. People are hearing the gospel message.

They are giving themselves as living sacrifices to God and are being changed. There is great joy.[13]

King David's prayer—and, I hope, your prayer and mine—is being answered:

May the peoples praise you, O God; may all the peoples praise you.

May the nations be glad and sing for joy,

---

[13] See, for instance, John Maust, *New Song in the Andes* (Pasadena, CA: William Carey Library Publishers, 1992).

for you rule the people justly and guide the nations of the earth.
—Psalm 67:3-4

Questions

- Looking back on what we've read, what do you think were the *good* things about the Incan, Aztec, and Mayan cultures? What were the *bad* things?
- What do you wish you could learn more about?

Bibliography

* Baudez, Claude and Sydney Picasso; Caroline Palmer, Trans. *Lost Cities of the Maya* (New York, NY: Harry N. Abrams, Inc., 1992). Fascinating account of the history of the discovery of Mayan civilizations by European explorers. Small print.

* Bray, Warwick. *Everyday Life of the Aztecs* (New York: Dorset Press, 1987). Excellent basic text on the subject.

Burrell, Roy. *Life in the Time of Moctezuma and the Aztecs* (Austin, TX: Raintree Steck-Vaughn Publishers, 1993).

Bushnell, G.H.S. *Peru* (Nottingham, England: Thomas Forman and Sons, Ltd., 1957).

Carrasco, David and Eduardo Matos Moctezuma. *Moctezuma's Mexico: Visions of the Aztec World* (Niwot, CO: University Press of Colorado, 1992).

Greene, Jacqueline D. *The Maya* (New York, NY: Franklin Watts, 1992).

* Marrin, Albert, *Aztecs and Spaniards* (New York: Atheneum, 1986). Excellent portrayal of the fall of the Aztec Empire.

* Meyer, Carolyn and Charles Gallenkamp. *The Mystery of the Ancient Maya* (New York, NY: Atheneum, 1985). A thorough study of the Mayans presented in the form of an adventure/discovery book.

Moctezuma, Eduardo Matos. *The Aztecs* (New York, NY: Rizzoli International Publications, 1989).

Morison, Samuel Eliot. *Admiral of the Ocean Sea: A Life of Christopher Columbus* (Boston, MA: Little, Brown and Company, 1970 [1942]).

Moseley, Michael E. *The Incas and Their Ancestors: The Archaeology of Peru* (New York, NY: Thames and Hudson, 1992).

Noakes, Greg. "The Other 1492," *Aramco World*, January-February 1993, Vol. 44, No. 1, pp. 2-10.

* Powell, Philip Wayne. *Tree of Hate* (New York, NY: Basic Books, 1971). Excellent counter-balance to the "Black Legend" of Spaniards' special culpability.

Prescott, William H. *The Incas* (New York, NY: Crescent Books, 1981).

* Roberts, David. *Lost City of the Incas* (New York, NY: Rand McNally & Company, 1977). Easy-to-read, yet thorough description of the Incans' culture and its demise.

Stuart, Gene S. and George E. Stuart. *Lost Kingdoms of the Maya* (Washington, DC: National Geographic Society, 1993).

Stuart, Gene S. and Mark Godfrey. *The Mighty Aztecs* (Washington, DC: National Geographic Society, 1981).

Time-Life Books, Editors of. *Aztecs: Reign of Blood & Splendor* (Alexandria, VA: Time-Life Books, 1992).

* Whitlock, Ralph. *Everyday Life of the Maya* (New York, NY: Dorset Press, 1987). Excellent basic text on the subject.

* More significant text.